Eileen
Fisher

EMBRACED *by the*
Holy Spirit

An Experience in
the Supernatural

Destiny Image₀ Publishers, Inc.
P.O. Box 310
Shippensburg, PA 17257-0310

*"Speaking to the Purposes of God for This Generation
and for the Generations to Come"*

ISBN 0-7684-2342-2

For Worldwide Distribution
Printed in the U.S.A.

This book and all other Destiny Image, Revival Press, MercyPlace,
Fresh Bread, Destiny Image Fiction, and Treasure House books are available
at Christian bookstores and distributors worldwide.

1 2 3 4 5 6 7 8 / 09 08 07 06 05

For a U.S. bookstore nearest you, call
1-800-722-6774.

For more information on foreign distributors, call
717-532-3040.

Or reach us on the Internet:
www.destinyimage.com

Dedication

To my husband, Fred, my protector and my love. You have carried my heart in yours and always will.

To my parents, Bernard and Ruth Flanigan, who gave me the example of prayer by being on their knees each night before they went to bed.

To my brothers, Bob, Jerry, David, Tim, and Willy, and my sisters, Rosemary, Ruthie, Lenora, and Liz, who helped put our parents on their knees before they went to bed.

To my children: My son, Michael, who will always be my first gift from heaven and I know you love it there now. To my only daughter, Theresa, who I fell deeply in love with on first sight and will never fall out of love with. You are my hero.

To my son-in-law, Michael, who is a trophy sent from above.

To my grandchildren: Garrett, the love of my life, and Gabrielle, my treasured gift from above. To Chris, my strong man, and Richard, my very first-born grandchild.

Acknowledgments

I would first like to thank the Father, the Son, and the Holy Spirit, for without them there would be no reason for this book. The faithful persistence of my friend the Holy Spirit who kept me and others going, even when we wanted to stop.

To Sharon, Linda, Sandy, Karen, Shirley, Marylou, Julie, and Diane, who helped me in so many ways in the preparation of this book, you are very much loved and appreciated.

Thank you, David Manuel, for pouring your incredible talent and wisdom into the book to help me "look good" and to keep God smiling.

I'd like to thank my pastor, Ted Haggard, for all the years of love, support, and encouragement he has given to me. You are my favorite pastor.

To Benny Hinn: God mightily used you to start me on a life-changing journey.

Contents

Introduction

Eileen Fisher has the funniest sense of humor of any woman I know. For reasons of His own, God has chosen to gift her with holy humor. I think I know what one of those reasons is. As she perpetually pokes fun at herself, making herself look ridiculous whenever she gets stuck in a sin, she invites us to join her in laughing at herself—sometimes getting us laughing so hard that we beg her to stop.

And pretty soon we see how ridiculous we are, when we get stuck in a similar sin.

It has been said—and sung—that a little bit of sugar makes the medicine go down. Our laughter at how foolish we can be, when we get stuck in pride or whatever, is that sugar which often provides us with some pretty strong medicine.

Eileen is calling on all of us, whether we have just begun or have been walking with God for a long time, to get serious about surrendering our will to His. She doesn't make it sound easy, but she does make it sound like fun. Joyful surrender. And her own imperfect example is what she uses to encourage us to try.

In this book she concentrates on opening our hearts to the wooing of the third Person in the Trinity, the One whom many of us know the least well, so we can become more intimate with Him. She shows us how He is the Enabler, the Teacher, the Comforter, the Inspirer, and the special Friend whom Jesus promised the Father would send after He returned to Heaven. He wants to help us do what is foremost on His mind: lifting up Jesus and glorifying God.

And if we are reluctant, if we are quite comfortable with the God we encounter at church on Sundays and really don't want to get any closer to Him, then the Holy Spirit, in His role as "Heaven's Divine Stalker," might gently but persistently pursue us, until we finally surrender to God's plan for our lives and receive the extravagant love the Holy Spirit Himself has to offer us.

This book, then, is the chronicle of a divine love affair. It begins with Eileen resisting the drawing of the Holy Spirit into greater intimacy with the Father. Then she succumbs and surrenders. And finally she wants to be enfolded in the circle of perfect love that the Holy Trinity represents.

And she makes us want to, also. As the Holy Spirit kindles this desire in our hearts, Eileen offers prayers for us to pray with her, prayers that will make it so.

This is not a book to read and set aside. It is a book to experience and enter into. You will not emerge unchanged, and you will be grateful for the change.

—David Manuel

Chapter 1

Are You Being Stalked?

A New Adventure

The main ballroom of the hotel in Seattle was packed, as my husband, Fred, and I scanned the crowd in hopes of finding two seats together. Out of the corner of my eye, I spotted two chairs in the center—a great place to see all that would happen! And yet I was not sure I wanted to see whatever might happen.

This was a new adventure for us, I thought as we took our seats. I felt intense excitement in the room, but I also felt trapped, for I realized we would be right in the middle of it all, and it would be impossible to leave the service discreetly if these people began to behave strangely. At least we could leave quietly, I noted, because no one would hear our steps on the thick carpet.

I sensed the anticipation of the crowd growing, and it became contagious. I felt it, too, but I kept reminding myself that I was free to leave at any time. Worship music filled the room, permeating the air like a sweet fragrance, inviting us to stay and see what God would do.

Everyone grew quiet; a holy hush came over the crowd. Yet, the atmosphere seemed to be charged with something like a vibrant electrical current, and it was completely different from anything I had ever felt before. My curiosity was peaking, but I had no idea what to expect next. Hope began to well up in my heart. Would God pour out His presence here? Now? In me? I truly hoped so.

As I thought about how we came to be sitting in this ballroom, all at once my heart was overwhelmed by the goodness and faithfulness of God. We had been on a bittersweet journey.

I glanced over at Fred. It didn't seem like his nerves were on edge at all. In fact, I felt safe and peaceful just looking at him. Always steadfast and stable, Fred never jumped on the "bandwagons" that came along, but he was always careful to test each situation that presented itself to us. My husband, unlike myself, had the wonderful ability to bring calm into the middle of any of life's storms. Once I researched the meaning of his name and discovered that it denotes a "peaceful ruler," and even during the times when I would try to overthrow his "kingdom," he would remain unperturbed.

Fred and I grew up together, and for most of our lives I had been testing him in his role as a peacemaker. I loved to stir up things and challenge him. Now, as I looked at him, I could see him as an 8-year-old boy and see myself as a 6-year-old girl back when I tried to hit him with a baseball, so we could all laugh at his adult-serious response.

Fred knew how to get even, however. When we were older, for example, he would suggest a game of hide-and-seek with me and my brother Dave. Then, after I found a good hiding place, he and Dave would leave me there and go off to the corner drugstore for a Coke!

From the beginning, it seemed that my assignment had been to get him to take life less seriously and to learn to laugh. On this particular evening in the ballroom, I realized that this was still my goal for him. I gazed fondly at him. He was not just my partner; he was my friend—a friend indeed, in this situation. I knew that if I felt the sudden urge to sneak out of there at any point, he would leave right beside me, and this was a truly comforting thought. I also realized that I was sitting next to my spiritual partner. I was confident that we could handle this situation, regardless of what might occur, because of all the other situations we'd been through together for so many wonderful years.

A NEW SEASON IN OUR LIVES

When Fred joined the army, and I became his wife, there were many times when he would travel to a new duty station ahead of me, and I would later, after a time of deep longing, follow him to our new home. Likewise, there were many times when Fred would return home from duty to find me still waiting for him. At those times we were not able to be together.

Now we were embarking together on a new season in our lives. Having just come back to the States from a three-year tour in Germany, we felt quite disconnected from others who were hungry for more of God. It felt as if we had been wandering in the desert for that three-year period, and we felt very isolated and thirsty. The truth is we were feeling very discouraged. It was our desire for a more intimate walk with God that had drawn us to this meeting being held in a Seattle hotel ballroom.

I reached over and took Fred's hand in mine and was immediately flooded with a sense of security. If the people in this meeting began acting weirdly, I knew Fred would know how to handle the situation.

Just then I smiled as I recalled our first date. It was a double-date with my brother, Dave, and his girlfriend. On that evening long ago, as we sat in the car discussing what we were going to do (we had plenty of time but no money), I gazed at the small mountains surrounding Spokane. There was an illuminated cross on the summit of one of these hills. Fred was 17 years old and he had recently gotten his driver's license, and he loved to drive. I suggested, "Let's drive to the top and look at that cross!"

How Heaven must have smiled that evening! Now here we were, all these years later, still going forward with the same message in mind: "Let's all go look at the cross."

On the night of our double-date it was raining, and the dirt road to the summit was muddy. I kept on challenging Fred, however, urging him to keep driving up the hill. This caused him to get stuck in a muddy ditch.

As the meeting in the ballroom progressed, I wondered if I had done something similar on this particular evening, because I imagined that the meeting could turn out to be another "muddy" situation. I realized that only God knew what the outcome of the evening would be. It was my fond hope that He would honor our decision to take the risk of attending the service and be open to His plan and purpose for our lives, but at the same time I felt very vulnerable, indeed.

But, more about that later.

STRANGE STRANGERS

While sitting in the ballroom that evening, my mind went back to another meeting Fred and I had attended a few years before without knowing where it would lead us. God's Holy Spirit was there, too, and He was moving and working in our hearts even though we didn't realize it.

The year was 1974, and we were sitting in another strange room that was filled with strangers who seemed very strange to us. This meeting took place in a school gymnasium, not a ballroom. We sat in bleachers rather than velvet-covered chairs. On this particular evening I surveyed the scene as usual, giving special attention to the exits, just in case I would "need" them. The distance to the nearest exit, I soon discovered, was considerable. If we suddenly had to leave, we'd have to excuse ourselves at least a dozen times, as we climbed over the other folk who were sitting in the bleachers. This realization made me very uncomfortable.

The group in the gym was small in comparison to the gathering in the ballroom. The gym itself seemed large, however. It was attached to a Catholic elementary school, and it had a familiar feeling to me, for it was like the one Fred and I had played in as kids.

Both Fred and I had been raised as Catholics, had gone all the way through St. Aloysius School, and had expected to remain Catholics. I was, in fact, probably one of the proudest Irish Catholic girls on the face of the earth. I loved my heritage and would never have dreamed of joining a different church.

Like most young Irish Catholic girls who desired to become more holy, I had even considered becoming a nun. At the end of eighth grade, just before graduating from grade school, I went away on a silent retreat with my fellow students. It was to be a time of reflection with regard to what God's plan for each of us was.

When I returned home after the retreat, I announced to my family at our dining table that I had been called by God to serve Him as a nun. Fred was at the table with us that evening, and he almost choked on his broccoli when he heard me say this.

He had (I learned years later) been secretly praying that he and I would be married one day. Of course, it would have been impossible for me to become his bride if I took vows to become a nun.

This must have made God smile, as He took notice of my zeal. He knew I would be far better off as Fred's wife than I would have been if I had been in a convent, giving the sisters and the Mother Superior great consternation as a result of my tendency to be a comedian in those early days.

God was preparing us for lives in His service, to be sure, but it would not be as religious in the Roman Catholic Church. Years later, as we sat in the gym—listening to praise and worship that was far from familiar to us—we began to hear Him calling us in a way that we had not expected.

Marriage Encounter

Actually, God had used a Marriage Encounter retreat that we took prior to this experience in the gym to "prime our pumps" for the possibility that He might have a plan for our lives that differed from our own—as hard as that was for me to believe.

The retreat masters told us that God had a joint plan for our life together as a couple. I dearly liked this concept. Who wouldn't want to be closer to their spouse and still be in God's plan? But, what if God's plan differed from yours, as is usually the case? I was all for His plan as long as He was all for mine. God was definitely in my overall plan, and I was more than willing to let Him stay there (so long as He did not require me to change in any way). Wasn't that big and gracious of me?

"HIDING OUT" IN CHURCH AND RELIGION

Until that night in the gym, I had not realized I'd been hiding out in church and in religion. Actually, I was hiding from God. Not only was I a good Irish Catholic, I would have made a great Pharisee, as well for, as you know Pharisees were well-known for their hypocrisy.

Outwardly, I had a well-polished appearance of righteousness, but inwardly, I had remained steadfastly oblivious to the love messages of faith and truth that surrounded me. God was always whispering to me, and He was sending messages to me from His heart. These messages had been written with the blood that poured from His Son on the cross, God was inviting Fred and me to come and partake of His Son's death and to receive His Son's gift of eternal and abundant life.

Even if you spend your life hanging out in a corral, it doesn't mean you're going to become a horse. Similarly, if you spend your life in a garage, you are not going to become a car! Surrendering to God is a matter of free choice and free will, and sometimes, without being aware of it, our heart attitudes can become stumbling blocks that prevent us from accepting His invitation.

I remember how Fred used to say, "The only reason I will go to Heaven is because I am so afraid of hell." God bids us to come to Him because of His goodness and love, not out of fear. The Bible says, *"Or despisest thou the riches of His goodness and forbearance and longsuffering; not knowing that the goodness of God leadeth thee to repentance?"* (Rom. 2:4).

That night in the gym, my heart was full of pride and arrogance. I was fighting the Holy Spirit and my husband's example. But, thank God for His goodness, mercy, and grace; He did not give up on me!

During the Marriage Encounter weekend I referred to earlier, I had made it my "mission" to make Fred become more open, but I never dreamed he would later become so open that he would surrender his whole life to Christ—leaving me with no choice but to follow suit.

So, there we were in the gym of a Catholic school, waiting for something that we knew not what like two ducks on a hot wire! We didn't know we were waiting to be "shot at" for the glory of God. Bang!! There went Fred. And, bang! There went Eileen.

In the following chapters you'll see what I mean.

Chapter 2

The Great Ambush

PURSUED BY THE HOLY SPIRIT

As I looked around the gym at the others who were sitting on folding chairs, I experienced a feeling of pity for them. They seemed strange and weird, even though they appeared to be full of joy and peace. They had an air of smugness about them, like they were wrapped in a secret, intimate love affair with God, who seemed very personal and alive to them.

They seemed oblivious to me, as I stared at them, mocking them in my heart. I simply could not relate to them at all, and I didn't really have any desire to do so. I felt comfortable with my level of faith in God. He and I understood each other, I reasoned, even though He seemed so distant from me. I thought that if I prayed harder, and longer, and if I was a good person, then He would love me. He knew I was trying my best, and He knew Fred was, too. We knew that if we were good enough and went to church enough and prayed long enough, we could "control" God.

As I sat there, I remembered an old saying I'd heard, "Religion is man reaching up to God, and salvation is God reaching down to man." We were religious, but maybe God was now reaching down to us. I began to wonder if we were full of religion, but devoid of His love.

I shook off that thought, however, and focused on the weirdness of the people around me. As the meeting began, every once in a while

I could hear people shouting, "Jesus is Lord!" or "Praise you, Lord!" They would lift their hands, as if they were able to reach out and touch God. This seemed pathetic to me, and I felt sorry for them, for I believed that if you wanted God to hear you, you had to have your hands folded quietly and pointed upward in a pious form. From my point of view, that was the proper position of your hands for prayer. Inwardly I chuckled as I asked myself, "Do they think God is deaf? Why do they have to shout? Are they trying to make God listen?"

To me, their behavior seemed wild and out of control. The way they acted made me feel embarrassed and ashamed for them. These so-called "charismatics" appeared to be very foolish people, I judged. I didn't know it, but self-righteousness was oozing from every pore of my body. I did not want to become like these "weird people," for I loved being an Irish Catholic, and I felt very comfortable in my religion.

The thought came to me that I had the fear of God, but I realized it wasn't leading to wisdom in my life. I spent a lot of time and effort keeping myself and Fred "religious." I knew all the "thou shalt nots " and " thou shalts," yet I never seemed able to adhere to them perfectly all the time. This was "my little secret," and I kept it well hidden. No one knew it, I reasoned, not even God.

I truly felt that Fred and I were "spiritual giants," and this God of ours must have been very well pleased with us. He could see our good deeds, and He knew how hard we were striving to keep all of His rules and remain in good standing with Him.

Just then, someone looked at me and said something in a language I didn't know. It sounded like this person might be speaking Spanish. Then someone else, who obviously did know the language, told me and everyone else in the room what it meant. The message implied that I was a sinner who had spent a lot of time in church and had found religion, but not Jesus!

My jaw tightened and so did my grip on my husband's arm. What I had just heard had made me furious! I hated being exposed in such a public way, and I hated all these people as well! I wanted to get out of there immediately, if not sooner! Right then! Therefore, I started to get to my feet, and I expected Fred to follow suit.

THE "DIVINE STALKER" HAD DIFFERENT PLANS

However, that wasn't the plan of the "Divine Stalker." I heard someone say, "If you need Jesus to be your Lord and Savior, just raise your hand." To my horror, I felt my husband trying to raise his hand. As he did so, I poked him hard in the ribs with my elbow. He responded by trying to pull away. Stiff with anger and fear, I muttered to Fred through clenched teeth, "Put your arm down! You came in here as a Catholic, and you're leaving here as one!"

About the same time I heard someone's voice urging, "If you want Jesus to change your life, come up front and let us pray for you."

I shifted my grip to get a stronger hold on my husband's arm, but at that very instant he shot up and abandoned me in order to go forward. I could see him from where I sat. They gently laid hands on him and began to pray. As they did so, he started to cry. The more he cried, the angrier I grew. I felt I'd lost my husband to Jesus and to all these "crazy people"! There he was, betraying me and making me look like a bad wife and sinner. How could he do this? The strong, steady man I had loved most of my life—how could he do this to *me*?

In the depths of my heart, I sensed that the "Divine Stalker" had won, and a new seeker had been found and was born again. At first, I struggled to dismiss this impression. Fred might have just been born again, but when he got back to his seat, I was going to kill him!

I noticed that he kept on crying, they kept on praying, and finally I could stand it no longer. I leaped to my feet and fled to the only private place I could think of—the ladies' restroom. At last I was alone, I was mad enough to "have it out" with God! I questioned, "How dare You do this to me?" The pronoun I used was not *us*, but *me*! I felt as if I was the victim of a personal affront, and I responded by screaming inwardly. My nerves were so raw. Hadn't I been a good-enough Christian for both of us?

Fearfully and smugly, I reluctantly prayed, "Dear Jesus, I admit I have sinned. If I have missed You in any way, please forgive me of all my sins and save me, whatever that means. I do love You and need You. Amen."

When no answer came, I felt I had won. They were all wrong! This rationalization made me feel that I was the only one who was right. Out of the spoils of the "war" I'd just won with God Himself, I felt very magnanimous, indeed. So, to make God feel good and maybe let Him save face, I would allow myself to be considered a sinner in some small way. And if, by any chance, I had missed really knowing Him—which, by the way, would have been, of course, through no fault of my own—I would now allow Him to come into my heart, because He seemed to be needing and wanting to.

My prayer didn't seem to work, however, and I felt nothing but complete relief at thinking I had been right—again.

But, as I put my hand on the doorknob to leave, the peace of God came over me so strongly that I could hardly see, let alone turn the handle. When I finally could move, I left the ladies' room no longer feeling fearful or angry; I felt simply overwhelmed by the power of God's peace and love.

I had just met Jesus, and I had been born again by His love!

When I found my husband back in the gym, all I could tell him was that I felt like I'd taken 30 Valium! It was amazing, wonderful, and I was experiencing incredible peace!

I told Fred what I had experienced in the ladies' room even though I wasn't sure I understood it myself. It was as though God, as my loving Father, was playing and pretending to let me, His small, weak child "win," just to make me feel loved. That was what my Lord Jesus did for me on this very special occasion.

It's very disturbing to think that if I had walked the earth at the same time Jesus did, I would probably have been more concerned about the lumber and nails that were needed to make the cross than about the One who was to be nailed upon it.

Once again, the drawing of my Father's love, in active agreement with my loving Savior and the Holy Spirit, had found a lost seeker, one who did not even know she had been lost and separated from God's love by sin.

Now, with a humble and most grateful heart, I need and always want to be reminded of the Word of God, which proclaims, *"For God so loved the world, that He gave His only begotten Son, that whosoever believeth in Him should not perish, but have everlasting life"* (John 3:16).

As you've noticed as you've read this chapter, I sometimes refer to my friend, the Holy Spirit, as the "Divine Stalker." I do so because the meaning of the verb to stalk is: 1) to pursue stealthily or under cover, or 2) to follow, track; drive, chase, pursue, walkup, flush out, ambush."

That is exactly what He did with Fred and me on that glorious evening. He stalked us and found us in spite of our resistance and pride. That evening I truly felt embraced by Him, and I discovered that He is a faithful member of the Trinity.

He gently woos some people; others, like Fred and me, He stalks, but His motive is always the same: *love.*

Indeed, He sometimes even whispers to your heart, *"Remember, God loves you."*

Chapter 3

Something New

BACK IN THE BALLROOM

Now, let's go back to the ballroom in Seattle that I mentioned in Chapter one. A sense of strong anticipation filled the air in that great hall.

I felt deeply touched by the music I heard there, and I had a strong sense that the Holy Spirit was at work in our midst and deep within me. In my wildest imagination, I could never have pictured myself being in such a meeting, waiting once again for the unknown to happen. I was wary once again, but I was also aware of a desperate hunger for more of God. How would my hunger for Him be filled, I wondered.

The Spirit of the Lord had once again become my "Divine Stalker," and, unlike before, I had become His very possessive seeker.

As usual, He responded in a way I would never have anticipated; He provoked me to jealousy by showing me how the meetings I had been conducting were lacking in power and how my prayer times with others were lacking in power, as well. As I was contemplating these spiritual revelations, God was leading those of us who were assembled in the ballroom into a deeper dimension of His glory than I had ever seen or experienced!

Though I was barely aware of it, deep in my heart, I was begging to be drawn into the love of the Godhead—the Father, the Son, and the Holy Spirit—the amazing and wondrous love they had for each other.

THE HOLY SPIRIT SPEAKS

I remembered a much-earlier time when, while I was in my bedroom in 1980, I felt the Holy Spirit speak to me, as He had to Peter on the rooftop: *"While Peter was still thinking about the vision, the Spirit said to him, 'Simon, three men are looking for you. So get up and go downstairs. Do not hesitate to go with them, for I have sent them'"* (Acts 10:19, NIV).

In my case, the Father, hearing the cry from my own heart, had sent His Spirit, who answered my heart's cry with these powerful words: *"My friend, I want our friendship to grow and grow, so that we are always together as one—one in mind, one in body, and one in agreement. I, too, desire that Jesus be lifted up. I, too, desire that people see and know that the Kingdom of God is real. I desire to know the love you have for Me and, in turn, have you know the love I have for you. I am your Counselor, I am your Teacher, and I am your Friend."*

I was very surprised by His message to me. I thought I knew the Holy Spirit in the same way I knew the Father and Jesus. Now the Holy Spirit had called me His friend! To think that He regarded me as His friend deeply touched me. Now I wanted to know the Holy Spirit in the same, intimate way that Jesus and the Father knew Him, and I began to hunger for a personal walk with Him.

I understood the power of the Gospel of Jesus Christ. But it was only as the Holy Spirit drew near to me that I began to realize what Paul meant in his second letter to the believers in Corinth. He wrote, *"But we all, with open face beholding as in a glass the glory of the Lord, are changed into the same image from glory to glory, even as by the Spirit of the Lord"* (2 Cor. 3:18).

When I'd given my heart to Jesus, I had experienced Him and received His gift of salvation. I'd assumed that I knew how to walk in the fullness of His power, because I thought it came with being born again. Yet, where were all the miracles? Where were the signs and wonders that Jesus had said would follow those who believed upon Him? Didn't He say He was going to the Father, and when He went to the Father, He would send us the Holy Spirit?

I had received the Holy Spirit. Apparently, however, I had not given Him total freedom to change me into a vessel from which He could flow, unhindered for the glory of God.

AWESOME POWER AND AMAZING MIRACLES

Little did I realize that I was about to see another human vessel who was more yielded to the Holy Spirit than anyone I'd ever seen. This man seemed surrendered to the point of total abandonment in his walk with God. There was no doubt about it, he was determined to foster an environment in which the Holy Spirit would be free to minister in whatever ways He chose.

Fred and I were very excited to attend this Full Gospel Conference in Seattle. We didn't care who the speaker was, for we knew we'd "come home." We were with brothers and sisters in Christ who were on fire with the Spirit of God. As you can see, my point of view regarding these people had changed!

Everyone in the ballroom stood up to greet the speaker as he was being introduced. We quickly learned that his name was Benny Hinn. I'd never heard of him before. He walked toward the platform in the front on the red carpet of the center aisle. As he did so, He extended his left arm, as if to greet each one personally. And, as he passed by row after row of people, they would fall back into their seats.

This seemed very strange to me, because I'd never seen the power of God flow through a human vessel in this way, having such an obvious impact on such a large gathering. There must have been several hundred who had congregated in the ballroom that night. Once again I found myself standing in judgment of others.

At least this time I was *standing* in judgment, not *sitting* in judgment as I had years earlier in the school gymnasium. As before, however, out of the corner of my eye, I located the bright red exit sign—just in case I would feel compelled to leave.

As I was contemplating my "escape," Benny Hinn came to our row. He paused, put down his left arm and extended his right. To my astonishment, row after row of people behind me and in front of me went down like a string of dominoes. It seemed like a weighty cloud of glory and power was resting upon them, causing them to collapse into their seats, but I remained standing!

What was wrong with me? How come I was the only one who wasn't affected by this power? What was I missing out on? I had that old, gnawing feeling that I was the only person in the room who was not in some "great secret."

I'd never seen God's power move among and upon such a large group of people in such dramatic and powerful ways. Somehow I felt connected and yet I remained disconnected. Connected, because we all loved and served and believed the Word of God. Disconnected, because the actions all around me were so alien to me that my mind was scrambling for answers, but it seemed like there were none to be found.

My internal conflict and questioning didn't block the move of God, at least not on the people around me. Yet, I now know that I was blocking the power of God from flowing into me, because I was not open to something new. I felt secure in my limited understanding of God's power, and I was comfortable with that. Even if it was God, I was still not sure I wanted to be a part of it. So, I just stood there feeling very alone.

As the meeting went on, however, I found myself being deeply touched by what I witnessed. For example, in response to Benny Hinn's invitation, an older couple who were in need of healing went to the platform. The husband looked very sick, indeed. Yet, when they were asked what they would like God to do for them, the man requested that his wife be healed (thereby putting her needs ahead of his). I thought it was a beautiful scene of love! And, as the power of God fell on both of them, I felt so helpless and alone. I was glad for them, but still felt more confused and disappointed than I had in years.

I knew from the Bible that God has no favorites. So why did I feel like His helpless stepchild who was unable to receive the fullness of her inheritance? I prayed for people, too. I, too, was called to go forth and heal the brokenhearted and set the captives free. Yet, deep within my heart, I knew that only a small percentage of the people I prayed for were being helped. And now I knew why. It was because of the limited measure of the Spirit of the Lord that flowed out of me.

Frustration, fear, and confusion formed a "team" within me, and I had joined them. It made no difference that everyone around me was smiling and laughing and excited. In fact, it seemed that the power of God got stronger as I withdrew more and more into myself.

So, I did the only thing I knew to do. I looked upon the scene in front of me with a very judgmental attitude, weeping inside while knowing that others were being touched in very obvious and tangible ways, by a powerful and awesome heavenly anointing. The Spirit of the Lord (I later learned) had been poured out upon us.

Eventually God showed me that the Holy Spirit lives within us, but we hold the keys to the doors that He flows through. If we lock those doors by grieving Him with fear and unbelief, even while in ministry, then we restrict the manifestation of His power, a power that declares and shows that the Kingdom of God has come to earth.

Early the next morning I was determined to seek more of the Kingdom of God. How? I wasn't sure. One thought that came to my mind was that I should pray. I reasoned that Jesus would pray, and I should, too. I cried to Him, "Jesus, please help me love the Holy Spirit like You do. Holy Spirit, Help me to love Jesus like You do. Father, I ask to be caught up in the same love You have for each other, so I can love You all more."

PERSONAL APPLICATION

Ask yourself the following four questions:

1. Do you desire to have the Holy Spirit become your close, intimate friend?

2. Do you long to be one with the Spirit?

3. Do you have a burning desire, like fire inside your heart, to see Jesus lifted up and for people to know that the Kingdom of God is real?

4. Are you a hungry seeker who wants to love and embrace the Holy Spirit, as He embraces you?

GOD'S DESIRE FOR YOUR LIFE

The Holy Spirit longs to call you His friend, just as the Lord did to Moses in Exodus 33:11, where we see the Lord speaking to His servant face-to-face, as a man speaks with his friend.

Let me encourage you to open your ears and heart as you read about the following things that cause the Holy Spirit to grieve:

"I am grieved by the words that hurt people. I am grieved by the evil that has people trapped, and by the hearts of those who follow after Jesus and do not allow the Kingdom of God to rule over their lives. I grieve when I hear words of unbelief that come out of the temple in which I dwell. It sorrows Me when I hear words of anger that hurt the people God has created. I am gentle, and a person who desires peace and order. I am a loving person who wants to heal and set free those whom God has made. I am a Friend to those who are lonely, and I always act like a gentle person."

Fellow seeker, have you been hurt by the words of someone you care for? Someone to whom you trusted your heart? Yet, in anger they broke your heart or the heart of someone you love? Stop and ask the Spirit of grace to give you the grace to forgive them. Or, maybe you need to forgive yourself. Perhaps some outburst of anger has caused you to withdraw into a lonely place, to avoid being hurt again.

Beloved, I ask you now to meditate upon this verse from the New Testament: *"Now the Lord is the Spirit, and where the Spirit of the Lord is, there is freedom."* (2 Cor. 3:17, NIV).

There *is* freedom from whatever you are going through—believe it! It is not God's will for you to live a lonely life, trapped within walls of pain, unable to feel and know His peace, power, and fellowship.

The Holy Spirit would speak these words to you: *"I open doors for My friends, and I close doors that would allow them to go the wrong way. I am always respectful and desire to have respect shown to Me. I am powerful, yet I am always gentle. I am able to fight for and defend My friends. I want them always to speak truth, just as I do, then our relationship will be one of trust and love. I am always faithful to them, and steadfast in My love for them. I will not disappoint them, but I will wait for them to ask Me to be a part of their fellowship. I treasure the time spent in prayer with them, just as Jesus treasured the time spent in prayer with the Father. I desire fellowship with every believer, and I want Jesus to be known as the King of kings and the Lord of lords."*

Do you long to declare with your whole heart, "Jesus is Lord"? The Holy Spirit wants to cry that out within you and through you. The Bible says, *"Therefore I tell you that no one who is speaking by the Spirit of God says 'Jesus be cursed,' and no one can say 'Jesus is Lord' except by the Holy Spirit"* (1 Cor. 12:3, NIV).

Fellow seeker, if your heart is burning within you now, tell the Holy Spirit you are ready to draw close to Him and to be led by Him in every area of your life. Tell Him you want to join Him in fellowship. Tell Him you want to cry out for the world to hear and know that Jesus is the King of kings!

And remember, the Holy Spirit wants you to trust Him. He is God, and He cannot lie. Listen to what He is saying to you now:

"I am not man, so I am not limited by flesh. I am Spirit. I love Jesus with a love that has no end, just as the Father and Jesus love Me. We share a pure love that man in his flesh cannot understand. We are always faithful to each other. The Father always desires love to flow in everyone. He is total love. He wants love to be made known to man. Jesus is love. He is also God and is always motivated by love. Jesus showed that love is more powerful than sin when He took hate and sin upon His body and changed them into love. Love is the most powerful way of life! Love sets people free and changes their hurts into joy. Love does not end, for God does not end, and He is love!"

"I desire that love be the total way of life for God's people. Only when they walk, talk, and act in love can they be free to help others. The love I give has no end. I am not limited by man, but I do respect the free will that has been given to them."

What will your response to the Spirit of the Lord be, when He declares that love is the most powerful force in life? Have you chosen to make love your aim above all else? Have you chosen to allow the Holy Spirit to prove His faithfulness to the Father and the Son through you, so the Kingdom of God might be spread throughout the earth? Do you choose to walk in a love covenant of agreement that He has sealed, one that the Holy Spirit can bear witness to?

If you have agreed to choose these things, ask the Holy Spirit to grow you up in love and into the knowledge of the love of God that has been shed abroad in your heart. (See Rom. 5:5.) When you were born again, you came to know Jesus as your Savior, Lord, and Master in an intimate and personal way.

Now, a word about the Father, who is the subject of our next chapter. As Jesus begins to reveal the Father's love for you, you receive this knowledge through the "filter" of your understanding of the word "Father." For some, the name of Father brings up a wonderful picture of love and security; however, this is not true for all, and may not apply at all times.

If your image of God the Father is out of balance or not in agreement with the Word of God, your walk with Him will be hindered. As you have already read, *"For God so loved the world, that He gave His only begotten Son"* (John 3:16). How is your trust level concerning God the Father? Are you willing to become vulnerable to Him?

God the Father wants you to experience His love in a powerful and intimate way, just as you experienced the love of Jesus when you were saved. Are you willing to let God love you unconditionally and change you as you grow in the knowledge of the love of God in Christ Jesus?

Chapter 4

The Father's Infinite Love

A Divine Appointment

When I was little, my father was the love of my life. He was a handsome and dashing figure, and the only trouble was that he worked on the railroad and was not home nearly as much as I would have liked. Whenever he had two days off, he would stop at my uncle's tavern on his way home and drink too much. But he was always glad to see me, and I was always glad to see him.

It was much later in life that I realized the effect this pattern would have on me. It left me with a feeling that at times he was there and loved me, but at other times he was far away and out of reach. I would feel neither safe nor protected at these times when he seemed so far away.

Many of us, for many reasons, have this in common: Our fathers were not there for us or available when we needed them.

One weekend I went on a retreat with Fred. The retreat center was in an old, white mansion and it was run by nuns who kept it impeccably clean. The grounds were beautiful, featuring row upon row of shrubs and large, spacious lawns to walk on, with a lovely duck pond in the back. It was a place of serenity and healing—how much healing, I would soon discover.

I had not realized how a distorted image of God the Father could hinder one's walk in His Kingdom. Your spirit might be born again, but your soul can still carry within it painful memories attached to emotions that can prevent you from experiencing the great depths of the love of God.

In His infinite goodness and mercy, God had once again arranged a divine appointment for me, this time with a visiting monk from Pecos, New Mexico. He had been invited as our speaker for the retreat, and he possessed a tremendous gift of healing. He would minister from the information that the Holy Spirit would reveal to him (the word of knowledge) in the lives of people who needed healing.

He taught us about the love of God the Father and how the Father so loved His children that He sent His Son to declare His love and reveal His heart. It was the heart of a God who *was* always and *is* always, and *will be* always longing to pour out His love on those He created. As the monk declared this simple message with the authority of revealed truth, however, I did not rejoice. On the contrary, as I had at the other divine appointments I discussed earlier in the book, I began to feel guarded once more. I thought, how could I or any other mere mortal ever grasp the knowledge of the love of God?

The monk spoke with such simplicity that it seemed too good to be true. As he gave Scripture after Scripture referring to and giving revelation knowledge of the love of God, I glanced surreptitiously around the room in my usual fashion. Some of the retreatants were smiling and nodding in agreement, but others were obviously becoming increasingly uncomfortable, as I was. Perhaps they were like me, not at all sure I could trust the God he described with the depth of love that the monk presented to us. I was somewhat relieved to see I was not the only one who was sitting with legs and arms crossed, back stiff, and brow furrowed.

Actually I felt inwardly divided. My head was agreeing with the speaker, because he was basically just quoting from the Scriptures. But my heart was pulling away. The depth of love he was describing demanded a response from my heart, and my heart was not at all sure it wanted to be that vulnerable.

The monk must have been aware of the wall of resistance some of us had erected around our hearts. He paid no attention to it, however, but continued like a man who was on a mission from Heaven. By the power of the Spirit, he was determined to spread the love of God upon both willing and unwilling vessels in order to bring healing and hope into our lives.

As he did so, more and more people were beginning to open to the love of God that he was describing to us. As I looked around again, I saw fewer crossed arms and stiff backs. In fact, there were now only a handful of us left. Then, looking right at me, the monk gently said, "If any of you are having a hard time receiving the Father's love, come talk to me during this retreat and I'll pray for you."

Once again, my heart was now pulling, but my will was resisting. And once again, my heart won. I made an appointment to meet with him during the afternoon break. I looked forward to it with a mixture of feelings. What if it didn't help? What if it *did* help?

Finally to stop the inner turmoil, I prayed, "Lord, make me open to receive all You desire for me to have. Amen."

That simple prayer brought peace to me, and making an effort to set all fear and pride aside, I made an appointment with the monk, then went to see him. I made Fred stand outside the door, just in case I might need him! What was I afraid of? Well, one scriptural truth that I knew really well kept coming to my mind: if you saw the face of God, you would die. You didn't want to "mess" with Him, for it could end up costing you your life! Look what happened to Jacob! He wrestled with God at Peniel, and it was only by God's grace that he lived to tell about it. Jacob said, *"I have seen God face to face, and my life is preserved"* (Gen. 32:30).

Leaving the door open, the monk smiled at me and offered me a chair. I sat down, gripping the chair's arms till my knuckles whitened. He came and stood behind me, but he did not touch me. Then he began to pray so softly that I missed some of it, but I did hear one part very clearly: "Father, show her how deeply You love her, show her Your great love for her."

I understood something intuitively then, something that my intellect would never have been able to comprehend. I became aware of the fact that the door to my heart opened inward. I realized that God could not push it open. I was the only one who could open it. My hand was on its knob, but fear was dripping from it, and I was trembling.

"Open it," my heart pleaded within me. "Let the love of God come rushing in!"

But I remained frozen.

"Open it!" my heart continued to cry. Somehow my heart knew that my false, fear-based love of God had to be entirely flushed out. I had to be washed clean and transplanted, repotted into the new, rich soil of God's unconditional love.

My heart knew this, but my will was still in command.

My eyes were closed, and I was terrified, as I waited for the face of God that would strike me dead—the face of a wrathful God, with long, white hair and fire in His eyes, ready to condemn me for all my sins and unbelief.

I waited and waited, and gradually I realized that there was no face, no voice. There was only me.

I opened the door to my heart and gave a huge sigh. I was still alive! And Fred still had his wife!

Now, with my eyes still shut, I began to see a small, puffy, white cloud coming toward me. It was like those clouds you see on clear, blue-sky days, warm and inviting. I liked that cloud! Yet it went right past me.

But now there were others, cloud after cloud, gathering in front of me, and such peace and the great depth of God's love began to pour into me, causing me to lose my intellectual attempt to understand what was happening. It was beautiful; I was just profoundly aware of His love for just me!

Soon I could not see the beginning or ending of the clouds. They appeared endless. In my heart I then heard the Father's voice speaking to me: *"Do you see these clouds? They fill the sky. They are just like the love I have for you. They have no beginning, and they have no end. This is My unlimited love for you and all My children."*

Next, the Spirit of the Lord whispered these words to me, *"I desire to walk and talk with each person and to open their eyes to the truths about Jesus, the Father, and Myself. I desire to work with them and show them how to lift up Jesus, so He will receive all the honor and glory that are His. He died on the cross, and walked through this world as a man, and He never knew sin. He opened the doors for all mankind, and now I want to show each person all that He did for them. I want them to see what His death on the cross purchased for them. Jesus wants each person to know what He did for them, so they can live the life that He alone can give."*

It was a divine encounter that changed me forever.

Chapter 5

Come, Know the Holy Spirit

THE POWER OF THE HOLY SPIRIT

After 30 years of experience with the Holy Spirit, I have gained a deeper understanding of what Jesus meant when He said, *"And I will pray the Father, and He shall give you another Comforter, that He may abide with you for ever; even the Spirit of truth; whom the world cannot receive, because it seeth Him not, neither knoweth Him: but ye know Him; for He dwelleth with you, and shall be in you"* (John 14: 16-17).

How did I come to know and love the Holy Spirit? I first had to realize—and admit—that I did *not* know Him, and was *not* sure how to get to know Him.

For anyone wanting to enter into a personal relationship with the Holy Spirit, the first step is to believe He is a person. As you and I do, He has things that please Him and things that grieve Him. So, the first thing I had to do is to learn what pleases Him and what grieves Him. To do this, we have to set aside time to be with Him.

Listening to His voice, then, is crucial, as well as priceless. One of the things that grieves the Holy Spirit is when we presume we know what He wants to do—without bothering to consult Him. One evening I was leading a ladies' church service, one that drew women from around the city. Some would come in laughing, while others appeared to be carrying the weight of the world on their shoulders. These latter ones would come in with their heads bowed, and as they sank into the pews, the sense of heaviness in the sanctuary would increase. How wounded they were and how they needed a loving touch from the Lord!

Earlier, presuming I knew best, I had decided that the Scripture and theme for that evening would be to enter the Lord's courts with praise and thanksgiving. Yet, so many of these women were so tired and heavy-laden that it would have been almost impossible for them to try to get up and participate in a joyful service.

My assessment was soon confirmed. Wendell Bull, an audio technician, was working behind me. Hidden behind the solid wood church railing, he was trying to put the sound system in working order. At least he was hidden for the most part, but once in a while he would look over the railing to check something, and then disappear again.

As this "jack-in-the-box" kept reappearing, some of the women began to smile, and their eyes danced with suppressed laughter. Others were too heavily burdened to see any humor in the situation.

As they all waited upon the Lord, I sensed the Holy Spirit was trying to take the service in a different than what I had planned. But, I was determined to stay on track with my plans until I became aware that the anointing of His presence was diminishing. As the service continued, the anointing did, in fact, weaken. So, I did the only thing I could think to do at the time: I told the worship team to sing more loudly. The louder they sang, the stronger His presence would be, I erroneously reasoned. It would force Him to move into what I wanted to do. But was I ever wrong!

I was guilty of an all-too-common misunderstanding. Extra volume is not—and never can be—a substitute for the power of His presence. It didn't work. It just got really, really loud.

Finally, in total frustration I turned to the worship team and said, "Let's stop. We're moving in the flesh. Let's wait on the Holy Spirit, and see what He wants to do." Doing this was somewhat humiliating, but peace eventually came.

And so, we waited on Him in silence, which is exactly what He wanted us to do. He reminded me of a related Scripture: *"Be still before the Lord, all mankind, because He has roused Himself from His holy dwelling"* (Zech. 2:13, NIV).

SENSITIVITY TO THE HOLY SPIRIT

The key here is to become acutely sensitive to the movement of the Holy Spirit. You must learn to recognize when He is rousing Himself, so that you step aside to let His movement and plan come forth. Many of us, not knowing any better, try to move *Him*, rather than let Him begin to move *us*. This was one of those situations.

As we waited, I began to realize He was drawing people to come forward for a personal prayer of healing, because He knew how much pain was in their hearts. He wanted to heal those hearts, but I was pushing my agenda, preferring to sing louder and louder—exactly the opposite of what He wanted to do.

He is not only the Spirit of stillness; He is the Spirit of patience, peace, and longsuffering. And that night His agenda was to heal the brokenhearted. Many times if we're not sure of the direction He wants to go in a service—or in our lives—the best policy is to stop, turn inward, and listen for His still, small voice. Far from wasting time, it saves time, and it brings healing, as He alone knows the greatest need at any given moment.

How important it is for us to guard against the sin of presumption! It is a subtle sin that emanates from pride, for it places my understanding, which is restricted and limited over His understanding, which is omniscient.

As soon as we made the change and went in His direction, His presence flooded the room! Tears began to flow, as broken hearts were mended. Then the worship team began to go into true and powerful, yet gentle and peaceful worship, which only enhanced His presence. All this happened only after I humbled myself. Talk about pouring contempt on your pride! But, as soon as we began to flow with Him, with His direction and His plan, we all sensed a tangible increase in His powerful presence. Now we were moving in the Spirit, by the Spirit, for the glory of God.

Sometimes, as children, when we demand to have our own way, we establish a pattern in our life of trying to out-yell the other child, to overpower them and win our way. It is a pattern that must die as we grow into adulthood—and into spiritual maturity. We must choose to prefer the wisdom of the Spirit of the Lord and be willing to set aside the wisdom of self.

Like any relationship, your relationship with the Holy Spirit can only grow as deep as you are willing to cultivate it. If you were to go to someone's home and they never talked or paid any attention to you, soon you would feel quite unwelcome. And not by what they did to you, but from what they did *not* do.

I sometimes wonder if the Holy Spirit does not weary of striving against man's will and the arm of flesh. That's how I'd feel if I were Him. But, He is an all-knowing God who understands us. And so, in spite of us, He still does what He longs to do. He still goes about showing that Jesus Christ is Lord and that the Kingdom of God is real and it *has* come to earth.

You may be nodding in agreement as you read this, but you still may be running your own agenda, your own meeting, and your own life. Choosing to yield to Him is an ongoing, daily, even hourly process. But the more you learn to freely yield, and give way to the Holy Spirit, the more you will sense His fuller presence. He is so willing and so easy to please. He is always totally on a heavenly agenda, and He is always inviting you to join Him.

Everything in life is either a lesson, a reward, or a test. That evening in the church was a test, and when I failed it, then belatedly passed it, it was meant to be a lesson, one that I would never forget.

So what happened? I forgot it! (I guess I'm a slow learner!)

But the Holy Spirit is the most patient of teachers. There He stands, in front of the blackboard, telling you that two plus two does not equal five, and handing you the chalk to try again. If the Teacher is really good—and there is none better—He will challenge you to rise up, stretch, and grow beyond your own limited knowledge or understanding.

Chapter 6

Is Anyone Out There?

IN NEED OF DIRECTION

Let me tell you about another evening service. It was one I conducted in Salt Lake City, Utah. Both men and women were in attendance. I had ministered at the same location previously. Everyone was anticipating a move of the Holy Spirit. Were we not all gathered in the name of Jesus? Surely the Holy Spirit would move in our midst as He had done before.

As I looked out over the packed dining room with its white linen tablecloths now covered with empty dessert dishes, I knew it was nearly time for me to begin. I knew the leader would be introducing me soon, but I had no idea what I was going to say!

Worse than that, I had no sense of direction from the Lord. From past experience I knew that when I did not have direction, the best thing was to be honest about it and admit it both to myself and others. It was better to look foolish for a moment than to be so foolish as to proceed in the flesh, pretending to be following the Spirit. We must always remember that it is not to us that people are drawn; it is to the Spirit of the Lord within us.

The Spirit of the Lord was present at this gathering, and He was expecting to do His ministry, not mine. So, there I sat, hoping, waiting prayerfully and fearfully—yet confidently trusting the Holy Spirit to reveal His direction to me. I sensed that this night He wanted me to "get out of the boat and walk on the water." This, I knew, would require supreme faith and being totally in Him and His plan. I could hardly breathe as I contemplated these truths.

I caught the eye of the leader of the worship team, and I signaled her to have them keep singing. She did this, but soon came over to me and whispered, "Are you ready with the message?"

I nodded, which was not exactly a lie. I did not have *the* message, but I could give *some* message, I reasoned.

They kept singing. I kept waiting. I was smiling, but inside I was frantically pleading with God: "Give me something! Anything!"

But nothing came!

When all else fails, go to the ladies' room! I got up and went to the restroom, assuring them I was fine and would be right back. At least I hoped I would be! The "water closet" had become my prayer closet of last resort. The Holy Spirit had rescued me there before, and I now begged Him to do so one more time.

However, He didn't this time.

After what seemed to be an interminable length of time, I had no choice but to go back into the banquet hall. "Just keep singing," I murmured to the worship leader.

Inside, however, I was screaming! I looked so ridiculous, not only to the worship team, but now people in the audience were beginning to frown and whisper to one another. But I knew I could not—I dared not—proceed in the flesh.

Finally, because I really had no other choice, I got to my feet and went to the podium. In blind hope, I opened my Bible and read, *"And I will pray the Father, and He shall give you another Comforter, that He may abide with you for ever"* (John 14:16).

This verse reminded me about the Holy Spirit coming to us, and in this situation I was desperately hoping that He would!

I finished reading the verse and waited. Nothing happened. Well, not entirely nothing. I sensed that the Holy Spirit was doing this on purpose. He was teaching me to yield in public, no matter how painful or embarrassing it might be. Was I willing to suffer public humiliation rather than compromise? My entire ministry seemed to be balanced on the fulcrum of that moment.

The worship team was almost as anxious and embarrassed as I was. But I refused to go in a direction that was not His.

Silence reigned.

Then I did something I had never done before. I asked the audience, "Is there anyone out there who has a question for God?"

The room became so still that the drop of the proverbial pin would have been easily audible. And all eyes were fixed on me; it was as if my hair had just turned green! They seemed to be in a state of shock. I imagined some were thinking, "Is she looking to them for the message, rather than bringing it herself?"

Then I thought I heard a heavy sigh in the room, which I interpreted to mean, "Why have we come? This meeting will only end in more disappointment."

A PROBING QUESTION

I waited for a few moments, then breathed a heavy sigh myself —it was a sigh of relief. Toward the back of the room, a young, thin girl stood up. She had light-brown hair and eyes that seemed empty, yet there was a faint flicker of hope emanating from somewhere deep within her soul. With a trembling, weak voice that was on the verge of breaking, she asked, "What do you do when you think God has forgotten you?"

She was fighting back tears, and instantly had the sympathy of most, if not all, of those present. Many others, I sensed, could have asked that question if they'd had the courage. In that moment the banquet hall was transformed. We had just eaten a sumptuous, joyful dinner, but now it seemed as if we were at a banquet of pain and mourning.

When Jesus comes to a banquet, however, He has no concern for what the master of ceremonies might have planned for the occasion. He knows exactly what is needed, and He always speaks to those needs. He will turn water into wine, if need be, and He will fill a broken heart with His love.

In my heart, not my head, I knew that He was about to turn ashes into joy, despair into hope, and pain and sickness into healing. This was to be His message for the evening. Unbeknownst to this girl, who was standing there frail and trembling, God was about to dry her tears and restore her faith. Because the Spirit of the Lord was now moving through the room, her question would be answered with the wisdom of God.

Now, as I began to try to answer her question, I smiled, because I knew the anointing of the Holy Spirit was back! I could speak boldly and confidently now, knowing that He was in control and giving me the words as I needed them. Praise you, dear Lord!

I went on to answer the young lady's question with an answer that was filled with hope. And, as I began to teach, the presence of God's Spirit increased. Tears began to flow freely, and I could feel the pain in the hearts of God's people, accumulated pain from experiences of isolation and rejection. I listened with awe, as the Holy Spirit, through me, melted hearts, renewed minds, and refreshed spirits.

At the end of the message I asked, "Is there anyone who wants to come forward for a fresh touch of God, to be encouraged and strengthened and filled with His presence?"

The whole room responded. And never before had I known so utterly and completely that it was all Him, and nothing of me. All I had done was to get out of His way.

How about you? Do you desire a fresh touch from God? Would you like Him to encourage and strengthen you, to fill you afresh with His presence?

God is the same now as He was that night. Indeed, He is the same yesterday, today and forever. (See Heb. 13:8.) Wherever you are right now, God's presence is beside you. The same Holy Spirit that hovered in the dining room that evening is hovering over you now. He longs to refill you and refresh you. If you would like Him to do so, pray the following prayer:

Heavenly Father, I would ask you right now, in the name of Jesus, to come and fill me with the presence of your Holy Spirit. I ask You to strengthen and refresh me. I ask that You would release and impart the gift of hope like fresh fire within me, that I, too, might exchange my sorrows for joy, my sickness for healing, my fears for faith, and my will for Your will. Fill me afresh to overflowing. Break off all isolation, rejection, and discouragement. Fill me with the sweetness of Your holy presence. I thank You, Father, that You have heard my prayer, and I receive its answer now. Come, Holy Spirit; I want to know You. Lord Jesus, fill me with Your Holy Spirit now.

Now that you have prayed, I would encourage you to be still and give the Holy Spirit time to answer your prayer and grant your heart's desire to you—to come to know Him and His presence in a deeper and more intimate way.

Chapter 7

Dwelling With the Holy Spirit

A Different Kind of Knowledge

Years ago, while we were living in Germany, I was teaching a junior high school class, and one of my young students was about to be confirmed. She asked if I would be her sponsor, which meant that I would be willing to stand by her and encourage her in her faith. It would be a beautiful service, where the bishop in his long, white robes, as well as a priest friend of mine in his robes, would go to each candidate and lay hands on them, asking that the Holy Spirit would come and fill the confirmands.

It also meant I would have to drive 60 miles to the military chapel where the ceremony was to take place. It was a beautiful spring day and the sky was bright blue and it seemed as if there was expectancy in the air. I was filled with great anticipation, knowing that this wonderful young girl was about to receive one of the greatest gifts of her entire life.

Unbeknownst to me, so was I. The Holy Spirit was about to break through and let me feel and taste His presence throughout the ceremony.

It was a solemn and beautiful service because of the seriousness of receiving the Holy Spirit. There were candles flickering and musicians playing softly and reverently, and there was a sweetness in the air, like the lingering fragrance of a vase of roses permeating the sanctuary.

My senses were on high alert, as well as my spirit and mind, because I knew I was in a holy place on holy ground, and I was about to observe a holy work. The realization filled my eyes with tears, and I am not usually a weeper. What's going on, I wondered, as I dabbed the corners of my eyes with a handkerchief. Why am I feeling this way on such a beautiful day?

Then my friend, the Holy Spirit, spoke to my heart: *"I will come and dwell with them, but few will ever allow me to flow out of them."* He is so honorable that He honored the priests' request. He also knew that some of the young people whose lives He was entering would never learn to hear His voice or recognize His presence and yield to Him. That afternoon He allowed me to feel His disappointment and grief over this situation. It was as if I was watching soldiers who were marching off to war, leaderless, with no one to guide or protect them. But these weren't even soldiers; they were just young children, and they were being sent off to face a well-trained adult army. They had no idea what they would be up against, and they had no counselor to aid them in understanding.

They did not really know the One they were receiving nor did they understand what He brought with Him and had to offer them. He longed to be their Counselor and he longed to lead, guide, and protect them. It wasn't their fault, really; no one had explained to them who this Person truly was.

Any attempt to explain could only go so far. It would be like trying to explain a rose to someone who'd never seen one. You could describe its lustrous beauty, its gentle fragrance, the sharp thorns on its stem, and the velvet smoothness of each petal. And they might gain some appreciation of it, probably more from your enthusiasm about what you were describing than from any of the details. But if you were to hand them a rose it would be an enticingly different experience.

So it is with the Holy Spirit. You can tell of His deeds and desires, but there's a huge difference between trying to describe Him intellectually, and praying and having someone receive Him and experience Him. It's the same thing with introducing someone to Jesus. All description pales in comparison to their asking Him to forgive their sins and become their Lord and Savior. In either case, it doesn't matter how much you've read or heard. Nothing compares to a face-to-face encounter with Someone who has been waiting all your life for you to realize how much He loves you.

The Holy Spirit is always moving, and He longs to share what Heaven wants to do on the face of the earth. He is looking for people who are ready and willing, even eager to yield at the cost of their pride, and to prefer His presence, so that Heaven can come. That is His heart's desire. He wants to commission, train, and raise up leaders and followers who will carry His presence and make known to all they will ever encounter that Heaven is real, just as He is a real person.

Jesus and the Holy Spirit work together, and they are a perfect team. And the offer of teamwork is made to every believer, to join the team and work with the Holy Spirit, who is the Team Leader. If you will come under His leadership, and let Him train you, as He reigns in your life, then you can help Him lift up Jesus, to a lost and dying world. That is always Heaven's agenda.

You can give a person a rose, but what they choose to do with that rose is entirely up to them. They can either throw it aside in the trash bin, or they can take it home, and enjoy it, smell it, and come to appreciate its beauty. So it is with the Holy Spirit. We can choose to set time aside and come to know Him, let Him become Heaven's enforcer – the One who enforces the desires of Heaven, letting Him flow through us and for us. The Holy Spirit wants to give us an intimate revelation of Jesus, who is the Rose of Sharon. This is a spiritual revelation that He is able to share because He has fellowship with Jesus and the Father. When Jesus prayed, *"Thy kingdom come, Thy will be done, on earth, as it is in Heaven,"* the Holy Spirit must have been bearing witness with Jesus and the Father. In total unity and with them in agreement, He must have shouted "Amen, so be it."

Jesus told us that the Holy Spirit abides and dwells within us. To dwell means to have a fixed abode, to reside, to remain, to continue in a particular state or place. The Holy Spirit remains so faithful to us "the blood-bought church, the bride of Christ," that if we were all to become aware of Him and the longing of His heart, the glory of God would fill every church and come forth *out of every believer.*

So many people live their lives without comfort, never knowing why they feel so alone. Could it be they have never understood it was not the plan of God that man ever be alone? Someone can offer you comfort, but if you do not receive it, you will not have it.

If only we knew how to receive from others. While it may be more blessed to give than to receive, it is surely more humbling to receive than to give. The reason may be that the one who is giving is the one who has the control, for he or she has chosen to give something. The one receiving must receive in submission, to the giver.

Then why did the Lord say it is more blessed to give than to receive? If you can learn well how to receive, the more you receive, the more you can give to others. Look at Jesus, the Father, and the Holy Spirit. They are always giving to us, always trying to bless us, so that we, in turn, can pass the blessings on. As we do so, Jesus is always glorified.

A Child-Like Father

When Jesus says, *"You must become as a little child to enter the Kingdom of God,"* He is presenting a key that will open the door of truth into the Kingdom of God. He wants us to take hold of that key and open the door so we will receive further revelation. However we can always throw the key away and stay in the comfort zone of a closed mind. I've done that in the past, as shared earlier. I was content to settle for a lower level of truth than the Spirit of God would have me walk in, along with a lower knowledge of Kingdom living. A door that is half open will give you part of the vision, and that was fine with me at the time. But the Divine Stalker (the Holy Spirit) would not let me remain where I was not when my heart yearned for all He had to offer.

In order to gain a full and panoramic view, a person must use the key, walk through the door, take hold of and embrace the wide-open vision. Pretty scary, huh? It is a risky choice, for a person must become vulnerable and his or her trust level has to be rebuilt with a new vision that is fully endorsed by and built upon the Word of God.

In order to embrace Heaven's view, we must see it with heavenly eyes. What does it mean to have heavenly eyes? It means the "I" inside me must step aside. We need to walk in absolute dependence upon His love, His faithfulness, and His loyalty. Only this will give us the view through the eyes of the Holy Spirit. Only in this way can we gain heavenly, divine ownership of all that is offered to God's people.

I have four grandchildren: Garrett, Gabrielle, Richard, and Chris. As you might expect I dote on them. If you have grandchildren, you probably do, too. When I give my precious grandbabies a gift, they don't ask me where it came from or how much it cost. All they want to know is how to play with it! How does it work? They are teachable (at least, when they're young). They want to receive, for they've yet to taste the power of absolute independence. Jesus said, *"Verily I say unto you, whosoever shall not receive the Kingdom of God as a little child, shall in no wise enter therein"* (Luke 18:17).Children feel safe in a peaceful, secure, and protected environment. The absence of fear gives them security and enables them to feel safe, enabling them to become "explorers" of the unknown.

To travel the unknown without wisdom, knowledge, and counsel is to place a person at great risk in a dangerous and possibly fatal situation.

To make a wise choice, the Spirit of wisdom and knowledge must be released along with the Spirit of counsel. Under the direction of the Holy Spirit, as we explore the truth of God's Word, we obtain knowledge from the Kingdom of God. And wisdom and knowledge are the very wings which cause us to rise up into the things of the Spirit, and into heavenly realms where we can gather knowledge and bring forth revelation for ourselves and for fellow explorers. To walk in the unknown, dwell in the unseen, and have our eyes opened, is to truly walk in faith. God not only requires that we become vulnerable and step out on the water as Peter did, but He would have us link arms with the Holy Spirit, as He shows us where and how to walk in His power and might.

THE HOLY SPIRIT LONGS TO TEACH US

The Holy Spirit longs to teach us, just as parents long to teach their children how to swim for safety reasons as well as for pleasure. Much training is needed in our walk in the Spirit for us to be able to swim out into the deep. To venture out without training is to risk disaster, even death.

The Holy Spirit would have us learn different "strokes," so we can flow in the different directions in which He is flowing. Some of these "strokes" are in the form of stillness, laughter, joy, conviction, praise, worship, and prayer. But, with each stroke, training is required. Extensive training is needed for us to be able to swim far out into the deep and to rescue those who are drowning because they lack knowledge or training.

A child with limited knowledge who lacks wise counsel, when given unbridled power, can cause great problems resulting in injury to themselves and others. It is, therefore, imperative to come to know the Holy Spirit and to know Him as the Spirit of Counsel. This knowledge is obtained through prayer. We must invite Him to enter our hearts and impart His wisdom to us.

If we choose to be vulnerable to Him we will be blessed. Or we can choose to remain closed to Him remaining limited in our thinking and receive little. When we learn to trust someone other than ourselves we may feel as if we are losing control. Much of this life of walking in the Spirit is wholly contrary to our flesh.

All to often instead of letting the Holy Spirit tell *us* what to do, we tell *Him* what to do. I have been to countless meetings where I have heard people order the Holy Spirit around, as if He were their servant, instead of the other way around.

If we really knew Him, we would not dare to presume to tell Him what to do. We would, instead, cry out from a pure heart, with open ears for His voice and His will to be revealed and accomplished.

God is looking for people who are hungry for a relationship, people who are seeking not only the power, but the Person who holds the power.

Chapter 8

Knowing the Mind of the Spirit

A Burning Desire

Do you know what the Holy Spirit has burning inside Him? His burning desire is to do what Jesus said He was being sent to do. *"But the Comforter, which is the Holy Ghost, whom the Father will send in my name, he shall teach you all things, and bring all things to your remembrance, whatsoever I have said unto you"* (John 14:26).

The Holy Spirit is our teacher, and He teaches us about everything! Moreover, He longs to pour out His teachings and blessings upon us, so we, in turn, can pour them out upon others.

One day the Lord told me He wanted me to host a radio show. I protested. Up to that point, the only thing I had ever done with radio was to turn it on, tune the dial, and listen. But He had made this clear to me: He was requiring me to go on radio and begin to teach, minister, and interview people.

I pointed out that I had no training, or knowledge in this area.

He pointed out that the Holy Spirit would teach me. He assured me that I would learn as I go—on-the-job training, as it were.

With a semi-willing and obedient heart, I decided to go ahead.

True to His word, the Holy Spirit was faithful in showing me how to proceed. And, as before, He taught me by letting me charge ahead without covering all the bases with Him first, and doing it the wrong way. This helped me grow in humility before Him.

I was invited to be a guest on a radio show in Colorado Springs. They asked me to write out potential interview questions in advance. They told me they would ask the questions I wrote down and all I would have to do would be to reply. In other words it would be a staged interview. The interview went smoothly, until my host repeated the same question she'd just asked me. My mind went blank. Having already given my answer to that question, I had nothing further to say on the subject (which happened rarely—but, for the glory of God, seems to be happening more these days)!

To fill air time, she began to read off the names of different nations through which the Spirit of God was moving. She was trying to give me time to gather my thoughts, but there were no thoughts to gather! They had all left my mind, and no new thoughts were arriving to take their place. So she continued to rattle on, until the show was finally over. To me, it felt like the longest show in the history of radio broadcasting.

Later, I learned the term that described this predicament: dead air. And believe me it really was dead! And it never resurrected! Well at least I would not be billed for it. I felt sorry for the listeners, for my host, and most of all, for myself. Lord, I prayed inwardly as I thanked everyone and headed for the door, "Let this be the last radio show ever. Amen!"

But, as I left the station, I also felt a nagging sense of conviction. What God had wanted to take place had not happened. It had merely been a show that was informative, but not one that was anointed. Pondering this in my heart, I heard the Spirit of the Lord speak to me. *"That was the wrong way to do a show. I never want you to do it that way again."*

As thankful as I was for His guidance, it seemed to come a little late—at least too late to save my dignity and let me keep my pride.

And then I realized that it was not too late at all. His timing was, as always, just right.

OUR GREAT TEACHER

Once again, the experience was not about how important I was, but to show me a greater lesson for the Kingdom of God. Later on, when I had my own radio and television show, I would benefit from this lesson hundreds of times over. God said, *"I want you to be free to invite Me to join you on each show. Let it be open. Freely let your guest and yourself follow Me and flow in My anointing, whether it be teaching from the written word or in conversation."*

And that was how I was taught by my great Teacher. He showed me how to do radio and television in one quick lesson. Always remember to turn the control over to Him before you begin anything. Stay out of control, and never take control back from Him. Just flow with Him and go wherever He leads you. This was such an invaluable lesson for me both for the broadcasting studio and life itself.

The Holy Spirit is always willing to teach us but it is hard to teach a student who always has other things on his or her mind or never pays attention. Could this be why He suddenly shows up to get their attention?

The Holy Spirit has the greatest mind on earth and His is a perfect memory. He is fully capable of bringing things to our remembrance, if we allow Him to and are open to receive them. Once again, the key to learning to flow with and in the Holy Spirit is to be a good *listener*.

A student can go to school, but if he or she is always talking and never listening no knowledge is gained, and he or she has missed a unique opportunity to gain wisdom. The Holy Spirit wants to train us, teach us, disciple us, and equip us to fulfill every assignment we were created to fulfill. But we must become attentive and solely dependent upon Him for the enabling we need and His divinely appointed opportunities. We must become persistent and let our persistence be the ribbon that wraps the package of His knowledge.

Jesus said, *"Even the Spirit of truth; whom the world cannot receive, because it seeth him not, neither knoweth him: but ye know him; for he dwelleth with you, and shall be in you"* (John 14:17). This is a personal challenge. Jesus plants a seed in our hearts for a desire to really know the Holy Spirit. What we do with this challenge is totally up to us. Each person has a choice, regarding how well they want to *know* Him, not just how much they want to know *about* Him.

I could spend a day telling you about my husband, Fred, but if you really want to know him, the best way to do so is to spend that day talking and listening to him. Out of that fellowship a lasting relationship could develop. After we spend time with someone, we make a decision as to whether we want his or her as an intimate friend, a distant friend, or a mere acquaintance.

From the beginning of time the Holy Spirit has chosen to stand with the Bride of Jesus, as we cry out together: *"And the Spirit and the bride say 'Come.' And let him that heareth say, 'Come.' And let him that is athirst come. And whoever will, let him take the water of life freely"* (Rev. 22:17).

Are you thirsty? Are you willing to come to Him? Are you willing to be vulnerable, and let rivers of living water flow out of your belly so that others, too, may come and partake of the water of life?

If so, then come and let us continue to walk side by side, arm in arm, seeking together a deeper and more intimate relationship with the Spirit of God.

A PERSONAL PRAYER

Now, let us pray:

My friend, Holy Spirit, I ask you to place deep within me that which is burning inside of you, so I will know exactly what you want me to do and what you want to do through me.

My Friend, I ask you to forgive me for all the times when I have offended and grieved you. And I ask you today, that you will come and water the "seed of challenge" that will allow me to know you and your will.

I ask you today that you would place deep within me the key to becoming a good listener, that you will allow your gifts to freely flow through me. I ask that you will provide divine opportunities and appointments for me through your knowledge, that I can declare and bring revelation to others for the Kingdom of God.

Holy Spirit, I ask you for the gift of a listening heart and a quiet mind, that you would allow me to see as you see, to hear what you hear, and to feel what you feel, so we can go forth and heal the brokenhearted and set the captives free, that Jesus alone may be glorified. Amen.

Chapter 9

God Has a Wonderful Plan

A RELATIONSHIP OF LOVE

What a wonderful plan God has unfolded to us! The second verse in the Bible reads, *"And the earth was without form, and void; and darkness was upon the face of the deep. And the Spirit of God moved upon the face of the waters"* (Gen. 1:2).

Man, too, was without form and void until God took from the earth and formed him. Before this man had no form and was devoid of a spirit.

In the beginning the earth consisted mostly of water, just as our bodies are 90 percent water. Could it be that man is not composed entirely of water in order to keep him dependent upon water, especially the water that came from Jesus' side when He died on the cross? God has given us so many examples and reminders—that cause us to look to Him for the completion of who we are and the fulfillment of what we were created for, which is fellowship with Him.

Consider for a moment a green Christmas tree, that is filled with multicolored lights and decorations. It fills the room with the fragrance of pine. Does this scent not bring forth a flood of memories? So God uses concrete things to remind us of the love He has for us.

Jesus and the Holy Spirit demonstrate a wonderful love relationship to us, they declare their love and loyalty to each other time and again. Look how the Apostle John describes it: *"This is the one who came by water and blood [Jesus Christ]. He did not come by water only, but by water and blood. And it is the Spirit who testifies, because the Spirit is the truth for there are three who testify, the Spirit, the water and the blood and the three are all in agreement"* (1 John 5:6-8 NIV).

I love Bible verses that speak of how the Holy Spirit stayed with Jesus as He died on the cross. As John wrote, the Spirit was there, looking on, and He was an eyewitness of the crucifixion. John called Him the Spirit of Truth, because He brings revelation of what He witnessed to us. He was there through the whole agonizing ordeal that Jesus went through, grieving as the Father did, and witnessing the greatest act of love the world has ever seen or ever will see.

It is precisely because He is the Spirit of Truth that He so closely guards the glory that belongs to Jesus. He knows totally, as no one else does, how all power and glory belong to Jesus Christ, our Lord and King!

When the Holy Spirit saw the soldier's spear pierce Jesus' side, did the water that flowed out of His body bring back to His remembrance how He had descended on Jesus at His water baptism? How painfully beautiful and bittersweet it must have been for the Holy Spirit to witness the Godhead's plan unfolding in this way, yet mankind did not really understand. I wonder if it was when the water came from Jesus' side that the Holy Spirit left to return to Heaven? *"As soon as Jesus was baptized, He went up out of the water. At that moment Heaven was opened, and he saw the spirit of God descending like a dove and lighting on Him"* (Matt. 3:16 NIV).

Fellow seeker, are you, too, hungry for the Spirit of God to descend upon *you* like a dove? Is there in your heart a cry that is reaching up to Heaven asking God to renew you, fill you, anoint you, and establish you? If so, He will send you forth and empower you to do what He calls you to do.

Another of God's reminders is one you may not have considered before. When doves mate, they mate for life. This fact from nature reminds me of how much the Holy Spirit longs for lasting intimacy and fellowship with us. He has an eternal commitment to the God-head, and He longs to make the same eternal commitment to you. He will cover you with His wings and hover over you. He will comfort you and teach you how to rise above circumstances with His power, in His might, and with His strength.

INTIMATE FELLOWSHIP

At all times He is close to you, longing to linger over you and possess you. He always has a burning desire to whisper to you, spirit to spirit, to let you know of His faithfulness and the eternal covenant the Godhead has made with you. He wants to give you the gift of Himself. And His one desire is for you to receive and open the gift He is to you. Like a bride offering herself to her beloved and longing to know the secrets of his heart, He longs to be in intimate fellowship with you, knowing your heart's secrets and sharing His heart's secrets with you.

Once you have gained such intimacy, the two of you have a joint assignment: He wants to declare the Lordship of Jesus, and He wants you, empowered and enabled with His presence, to show that you truly have and serve a risen Lord.

Do you desire to become a living, declaring witness, one with inner revelation, knowledge, and information that can only confirm and declare the power of the risen Lord for the glory of His name? If you do, then above all, you need to have a living, vibrant relationship with the Holy Spirit, a relationship that is so tangible, that you can feel His presence, know His presence, and long for His presence. You need to believe and declare the power of the Word of God at all times.

The Holy Spirit has twice witnessed Heaven opening at Jesus' baptism and at His death. And now Heaven remains open to all who call upon the name of Jesus. *"And it shall come to pass that whosoever shall call on the name of the Lord shall be saved"* (Acts 2:21).

When Jesus died, the darkness that was over the world before He came returned. Yet, the greater truth is that He is the Light of the world, and the darkness has never overtaken the Light. The battle between Him and satan was never in doubt, for there was no sin in Him. He alone could overcome satan, the prince of darkness, for us and for all of mankind. *"For God who commanded the light to shine out of darkness, hath shined in our hearts, to give the light of the knowledge of the glory of God in the face of Jesus Christ"* (2 Cor. 4:6).

If you are longing for the glory of God and the presence of His Holy Spirit, you must meet Jesus face-to-face. Once you encounter Him, once you look into His eyes, you will become a reflector of His light, a person who shows the glory of God. The glory that comes from the face of Jesus will be the glory that reflects from your face, now shining for others to see the Kingdom of God.

Are you willing to become such a reflector? If you are, then you must also be willing to become a partaker of Jesus and the power of His resurrection. This, however, does not come without cost. In fact it cost Jesus His very life, and it will cost you your very self. In losing yourself, you will find Him, and you will find yourself alive forevermore in Christ Jesus. *"For in him we live, and move, and have our being; as certain also of your own poets have said, For we are also his offspring"* (Acts 17:28).

In John 1:4 we read, *"In him was life: and the life was the light of men."* It is hard to believe that the crown of thorns pressed onto the head of our beloved Savior was turned into a crown of glory. It is a wonderful truth that the same glory that shined on and from Him (Jesus) would be the glory and lifter of our heads. *"But we all with open face beholding as in a glass the glory of the Lord, are changed into the same image from glory to glory, even as by the Spirit of the Lord"* (2 Cor. 3:18).

WHO HOLDS THE TITLE TO YOUR LIFE?

How wonderful it is that the Father, Son, and Holy Spirit have never given up on us or all of mankind. Have you ever wondered why? Perhaps the reason, whether we acknowledge it or know it as fact, is that they, as divine owners, hold the title to our lives. Through the gift of our free wills, we have a choice to give back to them full permission to possess us, to embrace us fully, and to make them not only our Savior but our Divine Owner as well. Wanting no titles for ourselves, we have but one desire, that they hold all titles to our lives. They become the bearers of our titles, and we become the partakers of their blessings as the Bride of Christ.

From the foundation of the world, when God said, *"Let us make man in our own image"* (Gen. 1:26) the Godhead had a plan. They put it into full operation that it might unfold in the fullness of time. Each one would do His part to make man in Their image. What is that image? It was and continues to be no sin, all love, purity, holiness, and all that Jesus came to show us of Himself. The Godhead is still perfecting those of us who want to be perfected. They all three agree and always will do their part to complete the task of full restoration of man, through Jesus, our wonderful Savior.

"For whom He did foreknow, He also did predestinate to be conformed to the image of His Son, that He might be the firstborn among many brethren" (Rom. 8:29).

People are offered the choice between Heaven and hell. Unfortunately, some sit back with their arms folded, weighing the offer. This is simply incredible!

Even more incredible is the fact that the Creator of the universe would walk with them each day, and they don't accept His invitation. This, however does not discourage Him. In His infinite goodness and love, God is always reaching out to mankind. He has displayed His glory all around us, but many don't see it. I've never yet met a person who could create the sun or the moon, yet the One who did, bowed down to earth, so man could reach Heaven.

Man has tried to humble himself, but true humility is when the glory of God comes, and man sees himself as he truly is. He also sees

God in all His glory, and recognizes his need for God above everything else.

Unfortunately, though, this realization may not last for too soon we become impressed with ourselves again. It's pretty foolish when you really think about it, but it is nonetheless true. Imagine a weed, that brags about its importance to impress a rose. *"But we are all as an unclean thing, and all our righteousnesses are as filthy rags; and we all do fade as a leaf; and our iniquities, like the wind, have taken us away"* (Isa. 64:6).

What hope is there? All the hope we need is available to us. When we "put on the breast plate of righteousness" that Jesus gave us to wear over our hearts we are able to identify with His heart. Why? It's because He has taken away our hearts of stone and given us new heart.

WHAT IS THIS NEW HEART LIKE?

It's a heart of flesh, which means it is pliable. It also means you and He can mold it and shape it into something new, a heart that is open and teachable. And because it has been given new knowledge and a new touch of life, it desires to be used in a new way.

What is this new life that the strong, new heart longs for? It wants to pick up Heaven's heartbeat and be synchronized with it. It wants to beat as one with the heart of God. All the love that is in the Father's heart for mankind now fills this new heart. A fresh desire for Heaven comes down, and this new heart can now be lifted up. It is now able to be used and is able to respond to the higher calling of Heaven.

Now, filled with joy and peace and gratefulness, this new heart cries out, "Come, Holy Spirit, come!" And at the same time, it cries out, "Abba, Father!"

The new heart's strong, loud heartbeat it echoes throughout the whole earth and universe. It sounds out new words from God's vocabulary. The words of this new heart declare that Jesus is Lord.

"The heavens declare the glory of the Lord, the skies proclaim the works of His hands. Day after day they pour forth speech, night after night they display forth knowledge. There is no speech or language where their voice is not heard. Their voice goes out into all the earth, their words unto the end of the world"(Ps. 19:1-4 NIV). This is an opportunity to let our voices ring out in agreement with His voice, declaring the glory of the Lord throughout all creation.

"Therefore, as by the offense of one judgment came upon all men to condemnation; even so by the righteousness of One (Jesus) the free gift came upon all men unto justification of life"(Rom. 5:18). What we try to do to perfect our lives is impossible. It is an unrealistic goal. By the time we are old enough to understand right from wrong, our track record of sin begins to be recorded. *"But thanks be to God, which giveth us the victory through our Lord Jesus Christ"*(1 Cor. 15:57).

Our precious Friend, the Holy Spirit, wants us to not simply cry out a cry of victory. He wants us to live a victorious life. He wants to join His voice with ours in a victorious sound of agreement, as we declare together that Jesus Christ is Lord.

The Holy Spirit grieves when He sees people that Jesus gave His life for trying to undo the work of the cross with their mouths. Sometimes we may do this without even knowing we are doing it. We may fall into a trap of thinking too highly of ourselves, or too little of the love of God. Because the Holy Spirit knows the full price that was paid for each one of us, He sees our true worth. He sees our potential as the beloved Bride without spot or wrinkle, reigning with Christ Jesus. The message of Heaven is for Jesus to have a Bride who sits with Him in heavenly places, reigning and laughing at the plans of the enemy. *"But the Lord laughs at the wicked for he knows their day is coming"* (Ps. 37:13 NIV). A loving groom can hardly wait to take his bride as his wife and partake of intimacy and close fellowship with her. He does not long to see a bride who is filled with pain, grief, agony, confusion, weakness, or fear. He wants a joyful, happy bride and the heart of Jesus is to show off a strong bride, one who is purified and strengthened by a visit from his best man, the Holy Spirit.

Chapter 10

The Setup

No Longer Ruled by Others

While I was in prayer some time ago, the Lord spoke these words to me. *"I will never allow you to let man's opinion rule over your life."* This was a very comforting word to me because I felt so protected and cared for. But then a real test came. Have you ever noticed how quickly some tests come? And how they always seem to catch you by surprise?

I was in charge of religious teaching in a church program at the time, and the term was ending. It was time to select a gift to give to our students. The chaplain in charge had chosen a gift that would cause these children to place their faith and hope in an article (not a cross) that was to be worn around their necks.

I asked him if it would not be better to give each child a Bible with their name on it, so their faith would grow in the Word of God. If I'd stopped there, the scene might have ended civilly. But never one to hold back when I felt strongly about something, I added, "I could never put a child into such bondage to a thing." Then I said, "What if they lost it, or it got dirty?" I had no idea, not even a hint, that this chaplain had been wearing one of these articles around his neck for many years. He became beat red and full of anger. Calling me a "heretic" and a "fake" at the top of his lungs, he ordered me to leave, and then he escorted me down the long hall and out of the building, all the while berating me at the top of his lungs. Office doors flew open, and people looked out to see what was happening.

Dazed and sobbing, I walked home in a state of shock. If I'd had any inkling he was wearing one of the articles, I would never have opened my mouth. (I've always liked honey better than vinegar.) At the time of the incident we were living on a military base overseas and my husband, who was at work, heard about it by word of mouth before he came home for lunch. I was still stunned though it had happened two hours before. Word of the incident had apparently spread like wildfire and I was humiliated all over again.

I knew the Holy Spirit was grieving with me. But I also knew that somehow this had to do with His "killing" the power of man's opinion over my life. When I was finally able to get still enough to hear Him in my heart, He showed me that what I was going through was working death to self in my life, in order that life in Christ Jesus could flow freely from me.

Though I appreciated this, I sensed it did not seem to move Him that I'd been deeply hurt rejected and left standing alone. This particular day had started out bright and shining, but it had turned into one of the darkest days of my life.

And then a shaft of sunlight pierced the gloom. A few hours later a young woman who'd been attending the Bible study I taught, showed up at my door. Her eyes were dancing with joy and excitement. "Guess what?" she cried with delight. "I got it!"

"Got what?"

"My prayer language! It finally came!" A week before we had prayed with her to receive the baptism of the Holy Spirit and her heavenly prayer language. Nothing had apparently happened at the time, but there was no question about what had happened to her now!

She shouted, "And it's all thanks to you, Eileen!"

I rejoiced with her, happy to share one of the most wonderful times of her life.

Later, when I was alone again, I had to smile. I have to admit that was a very loving thing for the Holy Spirit to do at that particular time. I felt lower than a snake's belly, and how badly I needed some encouragement. The Holy Spirit showed me a little of the fruit that comes from being poured out for Jesus.

He reminded me of what He had said before. *"Not only will I never leave you nor forsake you, I will never allow you to have man's opinion ruling over your life."*

And then He spoke a great truth that I carry with me to this day. *"Neither of them spoke the full truth about you, for they do not have it. One built you up too high, after the other had put you down too low and you in your emotions, believed both of them."*

That message sobered me quite a bit. But that was not all He had to say to me. *"I want you so free of man's opinion that you will always follow Me, do what I tell you to do, and say what I want you to say, so Jesus can be lifted up. As long as you look to man, you are not looking at Me. Only when you are looking at me are you able to hear me clearly."*

Living above fear was a very long, hard, painful lesson. It had to be. He knew what was in my heart, and what things would become stumbling blocks in the ministry He'd placed me in. Anything less painful would not have done the necessary work.

Sometimes I still fall, but His love and grace carry me on toward the standard He has set for me. Toward complete freedom.

Another thing He and I had to work out was that I did not really see the fear of man as He saw it. He never said I was stiff-necked, yet fear does leave you stiff and unable to hear in your spirit when someone is speaking. You can say, "I love you," to a person who is at peace, and they can feel it and respond correctly, but when fear has a hold on you, the response is not the same.

Fear can block us from seeing the full truth. Put in a position of having to choose between pleasing man or the Holy Spirit, man sometimes wins. I didn't choose consciously to resist the Holy Spirit or grieve Him at that time, but I knew that I could have. Sooner or later we all could.

That is why it is so important to get this issue settled in our hearts. Few of us ever purposely choose to grieve the Holy Spirit. Nonetheless we do at times, and I believe this comes from not having a sealed relationship with Him, which means living in total agreement with Him.

AGREEMENT WITH THE HOLY SPIRIT

How do we get into agreement with him? We need to spend time with Him, to find out what exactly He wants us to agree with. Jesus, when He was on earth, drew great strength from the times He spent alone in the Father's presence. *"My meat is to do the will of Him that sent me, and to finish His work"* (John 4:34).

It would seem that the Holy Spirit is waiting for us to seal the agreement of our will to His. Could it be that He is looking for a pledge from us? A pledge to do whatever He puts in our spirits to do so Jesus will be glorified?

"It is the spirit that quickens; the flesh profits nothing; the words that I speak unto you are spirit and are life" (John 6:63). According to Webster's Dictionary, the verb "quicken" means: 1) to come to life, 2) to receive, 3) to increase in speed, hasten, and 4) to show vitality. Clearly the Word of God states that the flesh (our works) profits nothing. That's Heaven's point of view. Ours, on the other hand is something like, "maybe if I try harder and harder, it will produce and work." How many have lost hours within the Body of Christ because of this difference? These lost hours are priceless, squandered with no thought of showing forth the glory of God. In my life I know there have been many such lost opportunities and hours, if not days. Ten minutes of the Holy Spirit's quickening power can do more than 10,000 years of man's work.

Can you imagine what a powerhouse the Church of Jesus Christ would be to the world if we all lived as if we really believed the truths of His word? What would the Church be like if each one of us stayed daily in the presence of God until He had dropped into our spirit His daily assignment? And told us what He intended to do with and through us? It would be a radical church, one that would be filled with power and life.

How much life and power is in the average church? How much life and power flows out from the average Christian? Is it enough to revive the dead spirits of hungry, searching people?

Ask yourself this question: Is there enough of God's power in my life? Power that comes from being in His presence? Power to offer to a dying soul, with some still left over to keep me alive in this life? He said "The words I speak unto you, are spirit, and are life" What words? When was the last time you sat in His presence and heard His words?

Busy-ness does not always mean effective, powerful production. It can mean I'm doing my own powerless work. If we do not already have the mind of Christ in a matter, we can be swayed to follow the mind of man. How easy it is to fall into the trap of wanting and needing to perform for man's approval.

God is requiring us to be a bride that has a single longing, for the smiling approval of her Groom alone, regardless of the disapproving glances the rest of the wedding party. If, on your wedding day, you know your beloved groom looks at you with eyes that are alive, full of love and acceptance, you become unaware of any disapproval in the eyes of other people. The reason? You are involved in a secret love affair, just between the two of you. And when joined together, you have become comrades in a secret.

The Holy Spirit is seeking for the Bride of Jesus, to bring her into the secrets of Heaven, and to draw her by His wooing into the secret bridal chamber, where she can behold the presence of her loving Lord and Savior.

But there is a necessary and unavoidable preparation required to gain entry into that chamber. It comes only after a season of learning to die to self and dying to the need for the love of man. It comes when the burning love of your Beloved consumes all the shallow love that man has to offer. Man's love pales in comparison to the light of the glowing, on-fire love of your loving Groom, the Lord Jesus.

UNQUENCHABLE LOVE

The Bible says, "Our God is an all-consuming fire." In truth He is consumed with an unquenchable love. He wants to put this fire into the heart of His Bride, to bring Him and herself into intimacy that will actually provoke others to jealousy. In that fire He fans the flame of His own love upon us, just as He did on the Day of Pentecost. He sent forth the flame of His love for His Bride to be consumed by the love of her Beloved. Any ashes from her old life are cold and dead, and need to be taken out of the way, so as not to pull from the strength of the fire of true love. God alone is love, and His love for us is an eternal love eternally consuming and embracing us.

And what of the left over ashes? What value can they be to a powerful, burning fire? They must be pushed out of the way in order for the power that comes from the fire to produce the heat that will bring the warm to even the coldest environment. They will cause the bride to feel safe, secure, and warm. The Word of God says that He gives us beauty for ashes. *...to bestow on them a crown of beauty instead of ashes, and the oil of gladness instead of mourning, and a garment of praise instead of a spirit of despair"* (Isa. 61:3 NIV). This is very powerful and true.

The heavens cry, *"And let the beauty of the LORD our God be upon us: and establish thou the work of our hands upon us; yea, the work of our hands establish thou it"* (Ps. 90:17). Since the beauty of the Lord is upon you, wear it well and come out of the ashes. Perhaps even now you are sitting in a pile of ashes, ashes from broken dreams, broken relationships, or a broken heart. Perhaps alone in those cold ashes, you have not felt the fire or the love of God fanning the flame of your heart. If that is you, then hear this: **He who has called you *is* faithful and true, and where the Spirit of the Lord is, there is liberty.**

I would say this to you, rise up! Leave the coldness of the ashes! Wash the soot from your face, wash your hands clean, and bathe in the fountain of His Blood! For the Word says, "There is life in the blood."(John 6:54).

From the ashes of death, rise up now and put on His robes of righteousness! Come forth and behold the beauty of the Lord, as He puts upon you His very own glory! He has not called you to be a chambermaid, to sit alone in isolation among the ashes of the past, whether they be the ashes of your own pain or someone else's. Take off the grave clothes and rise up! Enter into the beauty of the Lord!

The Lord will train you and raise you up as one of His children so you, too, will become known as a child of God, and an heir of salvation. You are one who is blessed coming in and going out, because the fragrance and the fruits of the Spirit of God have worked in you and are at work in you. He is more than able to fully equip you to do all that He desires for you to do.

The key point is this: Make sure you are doing exactly what He desires and is calling you to do. Do only that and nothing but that, no matter how heavy the load might seem, because if He has given you the assignment, He will always help you. Jesus said, *"For my yoke is easy, and my burden is light"* (Matt. 11:30).

We train our children to cross the street safely. We tell them to stop, look, listen, and look again both ways. We tell them they can cross when all is clear. The Father does the same thing with us, His children. He, too, has a red, yellow, and green light system. When you feel anxious or driven it is time to stop, look, and listen. When you feel peace, go forward, empowered with a direction. If you are in need of direction, remember that the Lord has already given you the provision you need. He has sent to you a well-trained and enabled "personal crossing guard," and you may call him by His name, the Holy Spirit.

You need only to ask the Spirit of God to be released over your life, so you may obtain direction, counsel, and guidance so Jesus will be glorified. If you feel you are ready to do this, first look deep in your heart, ask your Guide the Holy Spirit to search for any sin of pride or fear, particularly the fear of man that may exist within you, and to kill it.

Then ask the Father to wash away every sin and take away every hindrance. Ask Him to clear the pathway and go beyond your understanding. Ask Him to search your heart and try you, to see if there is any sin within you. He will hear and answer your prayer.

When you have done this, when your heart has been cleansed and forgiven, it will become a heart on fire, going passionately after your all-consuming God.

Most of all, pray! The Psalmist wrote, *"Teach me to do thy will; for thou art my God: thy spirit is good; lead me into the land of uprightness"* (Ps. 143:10). I hope you make this your personal prayer—never forget that God watches over His Word to perform it. It is a lot easier to allow God to watch over His own Word than it is to bless your own word without His direction. It is very easy to place our faith and hope in His Word. It only requires faith and obedience on our part.

God's Spirit is so good! How good do you say He is? You will discover that His goodness has no end, for His Word says that He is an "Eternal Spirit of Goodness," and God does not lie. (Eph. 5:4).

From His Word, here is another prayer for you to use. *"Create in me a clean heart O God: and renew a right spirit within me. Cast me not away from thy presence; and take not thy Holy Spirit from me. Restore unto me the joy of thy salvation and uphold me with thy free spirit"* (Ps. 51:10-12).

If it is your heart's desire to have a deeper relationship with the Holy Spirit, keep on reading.

Chapter 11

The Land of Christianity

GOD IS THE GIVER OF EVERY GOOD AND PERFECT GIFT

Have you ever walked into a room and forgotten why you came into the room? Sometimes the Christian walk is like that. We enter into the "Land of Christianity," and often we do not know what we need. In fact, we're so glad to be there and we feel so at home that we forget what we were seeking.

Jesus knew we'd need help. The Father and the Holy Spirit knew this, as well. We may know it to a limited degree, but certainly not like the Godhead does. I love how they place this desire within us, then they fulfill that desire *for* us.

Parents sometimes do this also. When my daughter, Theresa, and my son, Michael, were young, as Christmas approached I would talk about different toys, knowing I had already hidden those toys in the closet. By the time Christmas arrived, they could hardly wait to open their gifts. More often than not, the toys were taken from the Christmas list they had labored over, but not always. I had to make sure that the toys would be good for them, not harmful.

I love Christmas; actually, I love to give and receive gifts all year round. Most people love to receive gifts, and the givers love seeing the delight in the receiver's display. Likewise God loves to give and receive, and when He made us in His image, he put that desire in our hearts. Jesus said, *"If ye then, being evil, know how to give good gifts unto your children: how much more shall your heavenly Father give the Holy Spirit to them that ask him?"* (Luke 11:13).

I love to pray and worship, because such times are "life lines" for me. Sometimes, when I get busy (or lazy), I begin to realize something is missing in my life. What is missing? The most precious thing in my life, being in the presence of God, in fellowship with him. You'd think I'd know that right away; even toddlers know that when they're hungry, they need to eat.

Speaking of food, sometimes I think some people may prefer food over times of fellowship with God. When you express true love, you always want to spend time with the person you love, regardless of whether you're hungry, or whether the food is good or bad.

Spiritual hunger is a gift we need to seek from God. He desires for us to hunger and thirst for His presence. Like an appetizer before a meal, the drawing of the Holy Spirit can awaken your appetite to crave more of His "food." Some people are content just to eat the appetizer and never fully enjoy the fullness of a complete meal. However, God does not offer just appetizers. He offers full meals that can satisfy anyone who truly hungers for His presence. The Holy Spirit stirs up a hunger that nothing can satisfy but the fullness of His presence.

A HUNGRY BRIDE

You can share a meal in His glory, because you've chosen, like Mary who sat at His feet, to learn from Him, to seek His presence more than the food that has been prepared. There is a cry in the Spirit's heart that says, *"Bring forth a hungry bride into the banquet room and set before her a banqueting meal that will be served by the Holy Spirit through the anointing of His presence."*

Are you a hungry bride? Are you distracted by the food when you would rather focus on the guest of honor, the Lord Jesus? God is looking for a Bride who will keep her eyes fixed on Him, not on the things that are set before her. It is crucial for a bride not to live like a child with limited understanding of the bridal meal, which is the written Word. We must come to understand, as the Bride of Christ, We must long for the nourishment His word provides for us that our Groom is the living Word. *"In the beginning was the Word, and the Word was with God, and the Word was God"* (John 1:1).

We, His Bride, should not separate ourselves merely to eat dainties or enjoy appetizers; we should crave and devour the meat of His Word, knowing that in doing so, we are devouring Him. The Bible tells us *"And the Word was made flesh, and dwelt among us, (and we beheld his glory, the glory as of the only begotten of the Father,) full of grace and truth"* (John 1:14).

We can choose to come and dwell in the Word, enjoying its meat and being consumed by it. As we consume it and are consumed by it the living Word comes to meet us. We pray that God might give us the understanding of a hungry heart, so that we would follow hard after our beloved Jesus and find Him and eat and share the meat of His Word with Him.

Solomon writes, *"He brought me to the banqueting house, and His banner over me was love"* (Song of Sol. 2:4). To love His Word, to dwell in and partake of His Word, is to fully embrace Him. In His garden under His banner of love we become one with Him, in Him, and through Him.

A PERSONAL PRAYER

Here is a prayer for hunger and understanding of God.

Father, Lord Jesus, Holy Spirit, I ask to be caught up in the love You have for each other. I desire to know each of You, Your heart and Your ways. Your love and trust for each other is so perfect, and I yearn to be part of it. But I do not want to love You from a distance. I want to be in the very embrace of Your love for me and each other.

I ask to have ears to hear You speak to one another, eyes to see what You see, and a heart to feel what is in Your heart. I ask each of You to go beyond my words and mind and look into the depths of my heart. Carry me away and place me in the presence of Your fellowship with each other.

I abandon my thoughts, will, and ways to You, and ask for Your help and grace. Grant me a greater love for You, for I need all three of You. I ask You to enlarge my heart and spirit so I can respond to You now. And finally, go beyond this prayer and do all that needs to be done to grant me the cry of my heart, for more of You now and always! My soul thirsts for You, the living God; now let me come and appear before You. Amen.

Jesus knew this day of crying out would happen in each of our lives, sooner or later, and He made provision for it. That is why He prayed *"And I will pray the Father and He shall give you another Comforter, that He may abide with you forever"* (John 14:16). Now that you have prayed this prayer in faith, stay open and remain in the place of expectation, believing and knowing that God longs to respond to your heart's desire. Make this a fervent prayer on a daily basis and cry out in persistence. Then let the God of Heaven respond as He surely will!

Chapter 12

Where Is God?

OUR FOREVER FAITHFUL FRIEND

Jesus could see the Holy Spirit when I was looking for Him. He had already asked the Holy Spirit to come as I asked for Him to do so. Indeed the Holy Spirit is a wonderful gift that Heaven is waiting to give to each of us. Jesus knew the Holy Spirit wanted to come and that with the Father's agreement, He would do so. Jesus knew the Holy Spirit would comfort us, our Savior did not leave us alone so we would feel abandoned and comfortless. He sent the Holy Spirit to be with us always.

He has provided us with a now-and-forever-faithful Friend, the Holy Spirit. He knew I would need the Holy Spirit dwelling within me, to lead, guide, comfort, and keep me walking in truth always.

Life does change. It may get better, or it may get worse. But it goes on, and so do we. It is during these life changes that we have an opportunity to see what our faith is truly made of. So often we live in the appearance of faith, while not experiencing genuine faith. It is in the valley of testing that we come to know our true feelings about Jesus. *"You will never know that He is the Lord of the Valley, if you only know Him as the Lord of the mountains."*

Mountaintop experiences prepare us and strengthen us to walk through the valleys. When we are on the mountains we feel the presence of the Lord and trust in Him. In the valley, however, whether a valley of pain, fear, or a hard situation, we sometimes find ourselves wondering why this is happening to us. We may even ask, "where is God?"

The heart that proclaims, "Jesus is Lord!" knows that He is indeed Lord over *all*. If, as we enter into valley times, we do not know this key truth, we will feel lost, confused, and we may even think our life is out of control. God wants us to *always* know He is Lord over all.

After all what is a valley in the eyes of God? A valley is the land between the mountains. If a mountain stream runs through it, it is fertile land. In our personal lives, however, valleys are the low times. During these "valley seasons," the water running is the tears of His people those who are searching for God. He longs to pour out His Holy Spirit upon our "valley of tears," as we open ourselves to Him.

When we are in the depths of the valley, the mountains seem distant, we feel hopeless, and it seems totally and impossible to reach the mountaintop. It is then that we grow weary, feel faint, and grow overwhelmed by what lies ahead of us. We may even wander off the path and lose our way completely. Just remember God sees all of this.

In such situations the Holy Spirit would counsel us, "Keep your eyes on the Rock, Jesus, and keep on the pathway that looks like it has been walked on before. It is the path of His people. Look ahead. See? That is Jesus, He is walking before you."

And then, speaking for the Father, He would add, "I make no mountain too high, no valley too low. I see each person as he or she is, and as he or she will become."

He would remind us what we used to be like when we first stepped into the "valley of decision." He might even show us ourselves, searching, hoping, calling out, not sure. He could or would even help us. At those times, hope was only a small flicker of light that at times would grow so dim we did not even know it was there.

However, He left the doors open, so we could find our way. He looked upon our hearts and saw thistles and thorns that had pulled at our hearts and made them hurt. He saw the weeds that had crept into those places, where there was a lack of love and security.

He sees us walking around in our valley that has become fertile with our tears. He sees all the things that led us into our valleys—the pain, the hurts, the broken dreams and relationships, the disappointment, and the rejection.

How do our tears make the valley fertile? God wants us to have a broken spirit, one in which He can provide immediate help for us and make a difference *right now* in our lives. Too often we grow proud in our sin and the fragile certainty that we are right. However if we will lay down our pride, the Lord will pour out His healing balm of love upon us. He wants to set His people free and plant their feet firmly on the solid pathway of truth.

When we were first called to share life with Him, it was an abundant life. It was His garden, where seeds would fall on fertile ground and reap a hundredfold or more of good fruit.

If we would really listen, we would hear the Spirit say, "Taste and see the goodness of the Lord. Pray to see beyond the thistle, and to walk on a clear pathway, the pathway He has cleared for you, as He walked before you." He desires to heal your heart *today*. He will plant a beautiful seed of love within it that will produce faith and hope, not only to bear fruit in your life, but to bear fruit in the lives of all His people.

Taste and See the Goodness of God

So, taste and see the goodness of the Lord, for He is your Healer and Deliverer. He is the Creator of all hearts, and all life starts from Him. He is the Giver of life, and He is the Keeper of life, for He *is* Life! Now, open your body, your heart, and your soul and see the goodness of the Lord, for He is the One who always was, is, and ever will be.

As I began to teach and minister, I stood before groups and made statements that now seem totally foreign to me. I would say such things as, "If you had more faith you would always be healed." Before I knew Jesus, I had been in the valley of tears and felt that I had nowhere to turn. When I was in my 20s, I went through three miscarriages, experienced the loss of my precious father, sent my husband off to Vietnam, and had a total hysterectomy. This all happened within a period of two years.

I was lost in a valley of hurt, confusion, and rage, and I gradually fixed my anger on God even though I was not sure He truly existed.

Religion can only carry you so far, and your faith in self and man are equally limited. At that time I had no idea that it was even possible to have a personal relationship with the living God, and I had no idea that I desperately needed that vital relationship. As I saw it, my relationship with God consisted of Him knocking me down, and each time I managed to get to my feet, He would take from me the little that I had, and leave me alone, crying my eyes out.

After so many losses, I felt trapped and hopeless. I sought professional help from an Army psychiatrist, who had a strong but private faith in Christ. Each week he would listen as I accused God of being responsible for all my pain and the pain of the whole world. Arriving with a heavy heart and full of Valium, I would renew my mission to convince him that there was no God. In my bitterness, I was longing for him to agree with me, which would have been the final confirmation that I was right.

But without realizing it, in the depths of my heart my spirit was clinging to the hope that the psychiatrist would do the opposite, that he would show me the reality of the living God.

The doctor, however, remained silent and non-judgmental toward both me and God. As we sat face-to-face in his small office, week after week for more than a year, my one desire was to challenge his faith and move him into my unbelief. Deep within I felt I'd find satisfaction in at least knowing that I had a right to hold onto my anger. I wanted the freedom to stand before God with a clenched fist that was raised toward him in open defiance, demanding a showdown between Him and me.

It seemed like the ultimate irony that all during that time I was still teaching religion and trying my hardest to convince others and myself of the love and faithfulness of God!

After a year of my continuous talking, the psychiatrist received orders that transferred him to another duty station. Our final session was bittersweet, for I'd grown fond of this counselor who had steadfastly refused to be drawn into my vortex of rage and self-pity. At the end of our time, he did something he told me he had never done before. He wrote me out a prescription and folded it in half, giving it to me as we said goodbye.

When I got outside, I opened it and I frowned. This is what he'd written: *"And I will ask the Father, and He will give you another counselor to be with you forever"* (John 14:16, NIV).

I was absolutely clueless about what this message meant, because I'd never looked up a Bible verse before. Shaking my head in disgust, I dismissed this psychiatrist in my mind as being some kind of religious fanatic. And yet he'd never once forced his faith or beliefs on me. All he would do was ask me questions, questions to prime the pump, as it were, and my "pump" didn't need much priming. So many times with my face full of fear, and my eyes flooded with tears, I would pour out the disappointment and anger that had been bottled up inside me for so long with no place to go.

Now he was suggesting that I accept God as my Counselor. This was hard to do since I did not believe He was real. There was a irony in this that I did not understand then. I *had* to believe He was real if I was going to blame Him for everything. At the same time, I did *not* want Him to be real, because if He were, I thought He would be a God of judgment and wrath. Consideration of these options brought me no peace whatsoever.

However, the journey toward God had begun, and I was not even aware of it.

Different people crossed my path and planted seeds of hope and faith. They were pointing me toward the time when I would make a personal decision to ask Jesus to be my personal Lord and Savior. The sad thing is, however, that when we receive a gift, we sometimes become so involved with the gift that we forget about the people who helped to prepare us to receive it.

For me, the psychiatrist was one of the people God had especially picked to help prepare me to receive the precious gift of salvation. After he was transferred, I, too, was transferred—to group therapy. Unbeknownst to me, the leader of my group was also a Christian. And not only was he a counselor; he was a minister as well. Once again, God had placed the exact right person who would field my questions about God with calm love and truth.

I needed calm love and truth at that time. While staggering around in the valley of despair, I had turned to man's substitute for God—Valium.

Eventually, it got to the point where I was given a psychiatric evaluation. When the results came back, to everyone's surprise including my own, they said I had a great, sound mind! This news gave me hope, yet I was still unsettled. When all was said and done, the real problem was still glaring like a red flag in the wind, and that flag raised this question: Where was God, and why was He not helping me?

THE TESTING OF OUR FAITH

Many times when we are going through a time of faith-testing, our eyes seem to be shut to the people God has placed in our path or the circumstances God is using to pull us up into a living faith.

Then, all of a sudden, it clicks! We begin to believe and cling to Him, the Risen One, the Author and Finisher of our Faith. We begin to realize that He alone is able to search our hearts and try us and heal us. The same God who allows us to experience wounds is the same God who heals, if we allow Him to do so. *"See now that I, even I, am He, and there is no God with me; I kill and I make alive; I wound and I heal: neither is there any that can deliver out of my hand."* (Deut. 32:39).

What does He wound? He wounds our pride and our unbelief. He wounds our dead spirits in order to make them alive with His touch of grace and healing. He wounds our self-exaltation, whether we are exalting ourselves through unbelief, or demanding that He show Himself and bow down with explanations in hand, so we *might* reward Him with worship. Make no mistake about it, that is the sin of self-idolatry.

The first of the Ten Commandments is: *"Thou shalt have no other gods before Me."* (Exod. 20:3).

And so, to look to Him, we must humble ourselves in the sight of the Lord, and He will lift us up with His grace and healing. His Word clearly states: *"For I say, through the grace given unto me, to every man that is among you, not to think of himself more highly than he ought to think; but to think soberly according as God has dealt to every man the measure of faith"* (Rom. 12:3).

God has given us the gift of free will. We can freely choose to turn our backs on Him and wallow in despair and unbelief or we can take hold of faith and rise up on the wings of His gift of faith to experience Him and respond to Him on His terms. We can honor Him for who He is and who His written Word says He is.

The problem lies not in what we choose to believe. So, yes, He does wound us, and He does so to drain the poison of unbelief and disbelief out of us and to make room to pour within us His gift of faith. We must always remember as He told the people who were with Moses to remember that He is the same God who brought them out of the land of Egypt and the house of bondage. Today that same God deeply desires to bring us out of the bondage of sin and death and bring us into the land of the living. He wants our spirits to born again and made alive in Christ Jesus. All we have to do is make the right choice.

The desire of the Holy Spirit is to reveal to all mankind the works and glory of Jesus. He loves Jesus. He wants all of mankind to love Him as He does. Similarly, Jesus loves the Holy Spirit and cares for Him, exactly as He did while they were together on earth.

Now Jesus wants His followers to do the same. I am amazed that the Scripture that the doctor gave me was the prayer Jesus prayed. Jesus knows it has been answered and is still being answered for myself and for countless millions.

After I came to know the Lord, His peace was absolutely overwhelming! What a priceless gift! It was one that I needed far more than I knew.

We always have a choice. I love the fact that Jesus asked the Father to send the Holy Spirit to 'woo' me, and He truly has done so. He wooed me into salvation and is still wooing me in the journey called life. Many of us do not know what we really need, but He always does.

Chapter 13

Faith Shaken Yet Not Broken

SUBMISSION AND OBEDIENCE

One of the greatest gifts in my life is to have a friend like the Holy Spirit who always speaks the truth to me. I've learned that He has a wonderful sense of humor. When I once complained to Him about feeling old, he replied, *"If you think you are old, you are not old not compared to me, for I am called the Ancient of Days".*

About 20 years ago the Body of Christ was going through extreme teaching about wifely submission It was extreme to the point where it was totally out of balance with the truth. I wanted my life to be in order, yet I heard sermons that did not set women free, but put them under slavery, devoid of love. I know God is a God of order and that our homes should be in order also. I think it is fine to have one head, yet I also know that two heads in agreement and love can be a very powerful combination. As it says in Deuteronomy, *"How should one chase a thousand, and two put ten thousand to flight, ..."* (Deut. 32:30).

To be covered by a man who loves you is a wonderful gift from God. I do not believe any woman who knows she is totally loved, cherished, and cared for as Jesus loves His Bride, the Church would not want to, quickly and without a moment's hesitation, submit herself to such a husband. Scripture goes on to say, *"Submitting yourselves one to another in the fear of God. Wives, submit yourselves unto your own husbands, as unto the Lord"* (Eph. 5:21-22).

To submit to one another is to practice humility. To prefer one another is to become one in the Spirit. And did Jesus not pray that we all might become one? For any marriage to become strong and retain its strength, the partners must share the same goal. They should have one vision, to become one in Christ Jesus. They need to walk in agreement.

One year, around income tax time, my husband was busy and asked if I would make an appointment with a tax specialist. I made the appointment, but while driving there, singing and playing worship music, the thought came to my mind, if I did the taxes myself (though I'd never done taxes before), we would not have to pay to have them prepared. With the money I saved us, I could take my husband out to dinner for a surprise!

I made a U-turn and headed back home in order to cancel the appointment and do the taxes. I thought, won't Fred be delighted with his clever wife! But the Holy Spirit had a different take on it. In my heart He said, *"Obedience is better than sacrifice."* I knew a related Bible verse—*"And Samuel said, hath the Lord, as great delight in burnt offerings and sacrifices as in obeying the voice of the Lord? Behold to obey is better than sacrifice and to hearken than the fat of rams."* (1 Sam. 15:22).

I wrestled with this truth for about a mile, then made another U-turn, back toward the tax people, but I was pretty grumpy about it. In my mind I reasoned, how hard could short-form taxes be to do?

When I arrived at the tax office, a secretary led me to a desk where a lady sat ready to do our taxes. Then, in spite of myself, I had to smile. The name plate on her desk announced that she was "Mrs. Lord." Okay, Father, I get the point! Obedience is better then sacrifice.

The Bride of the Lord had better be willing to obey Him in all areas. The Word says, "Submit one to another" (Eph. 5:21) And after all, you can see the perfect example of that in the Godhead. Jesus submits to the Father, the Holy Spirit submits to Jesus and this is powerfully perfect, because their love is powerfully perfect for each other, and they are ultimately one.

The Holy Spirit is first introduced in the Gospel of John as the Spirit of Truth (John14:17). What we do with the truth is our choice. We can flow with Him, or do our own thing. Free will is always a major factor in our life in the Spirit.

VALLEYS AND MOUNTAINS

Like you, I really do love mountaintops better than valleys. I love being caught up in the Lord's presence. It does not hurt being up there, compared to when you are down in a painful valley, but He comes down to where you are. One time when I was in such a dark valley, I was trying to get my husband healthier by going on walks with him. As we were crossing a dry and dirty vacant field that was overgrown with weeds and dead grass, I stepped down and heard a frightening, chilling sound. It was the sound of my ankle bone breaking. It did not just snap; it shattered and hung down limply with the bone protruding out of my skin.

Fred, a few feet ahead of me, heard the bone shatter. I collapsed to the ground and thought I would faint from the pain. He had to leave me while he ran for help, fearful that I would go into shock at any moment. There I lay; fighting to remain conscious and nauseous from the excruciating pain that now filled my whole body. "Jesus, Jesus, Jesus!" I groaned, hoping He would hear me.

Someone else heard me and quoted Scripture to me in a harsh, cold inner voice that brought no comfort, only fear and doubt. I knew the verses; they came from Psalm 91. *"For He will command his angels concerning you to guard you in all your ways; they will lift you up in their hands, so that you will not strike your foot against a stone"* (Ps. 91:11-12).

I *had* hit my foot against a stone, and it hurt like it was full of tormenting pain, as the ruler of that realm knew full well.

Soon I heard men's voices, presumably firemen and police, calling to each other, "Where is she?" They asked as they searched for me in their vehicles.

What if they didn't find me? What if they ran over me? They were driving back and forth with their windows down, and I could hear the sense of urgency in their voices.

"Over here!" I tried to shout, but I could muster little more than a whisper and the thick cover of dead grass blocked any view of me.

Finally they appeared, and I heard them gasp as they looked at the mess that had once been my ankle.

"How bad is it?" asked one emergency medical technician who looked into my eyes with compassion.

"Jesus, Jesus, Jesus!" was the only prayer I could manage.

"Morphine," he said to the other EMT.

Hearing that, I sighed with relief, as they put me on a gurney and into the back of the ambulance.

The ride to the hospital was long and bumpy, and with each bump I nearly passed out from the pain. Finally they administered the morphine, and that certainly did help.

The next thing I knew, I was in a hospital room, looking up at the face of a young orthopedic surgeon. Tenderly he said to me, "This will hurt, but I must reset your bone now."

Sitting down on the foot of my bed, he said, "Now take a deep breath."

I did as he directed. With both hands he took hold of my broken ankle, pulled it down, and then twisted it.

I blacked out. Inside, I was crying, "God, where are you? Why is this happening?" Nothing seemed to be going right. The anesthesiologist couldn't position the needles correctly in my spine, and with each miss, my foot would jerk out, and he would become angrier and more upset.

Finally, as I was being wheeled out of the room, I was awakened by the mother of all headaches. And again, I heard the accuser of the brethren mocking me. He said, "Where is your God? Did not He promise you would not be hurt if you hit your foot against a stone?"

I was too weak and too hurt to fend him off, much less take authority and rebuke him or cast him out. Therefore, he continued to torment me.

Several days went by. A nurse came in to check on my wound, and as she cut through the bandage that dressed it, the knife slipped and she cut me. As I watched in numb horror, blood began shooting up from the broken ankle like a fountain.

Eventually they managed to stop the blood flow, but I was badly shaken. I confessed every sin I could recall, and then confessed the sins of everybody I knew. But there was no breakthrough, no let up at all. Friends and family were praying as well. I was exhausted from lack of sleep, yet I remained awake because of the pain. The few times I did manage to doze off, I would be beleaguered by demonic dreams. The whole thing was a time of unbroken torment, as if God had lifted His hand from me and was now allowing satan to do to me whatever he wanted to do.

Finally, on the morning of the third day, I heard the precious voice of the Holy Spirit. He said, *"Move into the anointing and receive your healing."*

How can I move, I thought bitterly; I'm flat on my back!

I shared the room with another patient who was a Christian, a woman full of sympathy and compassion. She looked over at me, and seemed to understand my pain, yet she was unable to help. As we lay in our beds, I could hear her television broadcasting "The 700 Club." The host was speaking a word of knowledge. "I see a woman," he declared, "and the Lord is showing me that He is healing her broken ankle."

At this point, my roommate came over and full of excitement she told me that she had claimed that healing for me. God was healing my broken ankle!

Giving her back a weak smile, I said nothing. She was a dear and I didn't want to abuse her faith with my lack of it.

At the level of pain I was experiencing it felt as if my head was in the relentless grip of a vice and I could not see the Holy Spirit working in the circumstances around me.

Unbeknownst to me, however, He was.

A bit later a doctor came in and said, "We're going to take you in for a blood patch. You will either get rid of this headache, or it will get worse."

While I wondered what a blood patch was, the Holy Spirit spoke to me: *"That is the anointing, move into it."*

Chapter 14

God Loves Worms

FAITH FOR HEALING

As they wheeled me into the operating room, I felt the presence of the Holy Spirit. I had not felt or heard Him for the last three days. However, I had certainly heard the gloating voice of the accuser. He said *"You say your God is faithful? He left you out there like a worm. You could not even crawl like a worm."*

Too weak to take full authority over him, I nonetheless retorted, "You know what, devil? God made worms! And I would rather be a worm that God has made than anything else! God loves His worms!"

It was not much of a defense, but it was enough for that moment. It was a point of truth, and the devil could not argue with truth, because he is the father of lies. He left after that and more peace entered into the OR and my own heart.

The doctor drew blood from my arm and put it back into my spine, sealing the spot where spinal fluid had been leaking. When I sat up, the monster headache was gone!

And now, after three days in torment, I was finally able to sit up. It was like a hush of Heaven had fallen, as the Father stood at my head. There was total silence. The needle had gone into the perfect spot for healing, and Jesus had heard my cries. The Holy Spirit was once again my personal guide, as He hovered over me and guided the tip of the needle to the exact spot to seal the leakage from my spine.

Suddenly I longed for a hot, refreshing shower. The surgeon came in and hardly even recognized me.

He looked at me with a bemused expression on his face. "What kind of work do you do?"

"Why do you ask?"

"While you were under, you kept talking about how Jesus heals and how you had seen Him heal."

The anesthesiologist, apparently an unbeliever, had sat at my head throughout the operation, listening to me speak about a Jesus who heals. I chuckled at the thought.

"My brother's a minister," continued the surgeon. "You sounded exactly like him."

I laughed. So, after nine steel pins, wire, and a plate in my ankle, and a leak in my spine, the Gospel was still able to flow through a broken vessel.

As I left the hospital, I thanked God, not because I was leaving, but because the ordeal was over. He had used it to teach me the meaning of real spiritual warfare. You can read about it and hear about it, but until you actually walk through it yourself, you do not own it. I learned that in the depths of that shadowy valley, even if it felt like my God had forsaken me, He was with me every step of the way. And now I knew he always would be.

A short time later, "Job's friends" began to show up. One said, "You're in ministry. The devil's people put curses on you. It's Halloween." Another said, "If you had enough faith, you could have commanded your ankle to line up with the Word of God and be healed!" So much for the encouragement of fleshly counsel!

Through these circumstances I learned that body, soul, and spirit are connected. When my bone broke, my soul might have followed my emotions into torment and fear, but my spirit stayed steady. That is why I was still telling of the healing of Jesus, even while they operated on me.

The Holy Spirit always declares the good news and faithfulness of God. While my faith may have been shaken, it was not broken. Why? Because He carries it for me, just as He carries me. And now, as a result, it grew stronger than it had ever been before.

Sometimes, like Job's friends, we're tempted to judge the faith of others, when we really have no understanding of their situation or what they are going through.

After that, I asked Fred to keep "Job's comforters" away from me. My ankle was coming along nicely, but my soul needed time to heal, as well.

No Valley Is Too Low for God

What had I learned? I had learned that the *peace* of God, coupled with the *truth* of God, can heal more completely in one minute than anything man might conceive. I also learned that the truth does set you free, and that there is no valley so low that the goodness of God cannot reach it.

Personal Application

At this point, ask yourself the following questions, and answer them as honestly as you can:

1. Is Jesus the Lord of your valleys, as well as Lord of your mountaintops?

2. Is your faith real, or are you living in the appearance of faith?

3. What is your valley? Does it contain any elements of fear, anger, pain, or rejection?

4. Do you need God's grace and strength to flow into your valley?

Now that you have examined your heart, open it up. Invite the Holy Spirit to come into every valley of your life. Allow Him to flow in and meet you at your point of greatest need. Make Him the Lord of all your valleys as well as your mountaintops. Ask Him to establish your faith, so that it becomes real and operational, a faith that can carry you along with His grace and strength out of your valley.

Ask Him now to break off of you any act, thought pattern, or habit in your life, that keeps you from real faith and leaves you trying to keep up the appearance of faith in front of others.

A PERSONAL PRAYER

Now let's pray:

Dear Father, I ask right now that the Lord Jesus will allow His healing grace, as well as the blood that flowed from His body as a result of the stripes that He bore for me on Calvary, to turn all of my pain, all of my fears, all of my rejection, and all of my needs into something beautiful, that He would be glorified in my life.

Heavenly Father, I ask that the Holy Spirit, the revelator of my soul, would search me and continue to try my faith, that it would be found solid and genuine. I ask that You would forgive me for judging other people's faith.

I now take my freedom and will not accept the judgment of others regarding my faith. Nor will I enter into competition with the faith of others. I will trust You to carry me in your arms of faithfulness.

I ask you, Father, for a fresh anointing. And I declare that, as the Spirit of Truth releases in me the anointing that breaks off the yoke of heaviness, I am free to run through the valleys, and to fly to the mountaintops—and find myself in Your very presence.

Father, it is Your face that I seek. I would ask You today to ground me and root me deeply in the faith that Jesus has planted in me.

I thank You for the gift of faith. Let me use it that Jesus alone would be glorified. Amen.

Chapter 15

The Gift of Free Will

LISTENING FOR THE HOLY SPIRIT

In Utah after a Sunday morning service some years ago, I was ministering to people and praying for them. I was trying to hear the Holy Spirit tell me how to pray for each one, but next to me was a woman praying for people in a loud voice "O Lord, help this person!" she would cry.

She was so loud, in fact that I couldn't hear the Holy Spirit, so I stopped and waited till she was finished. Who was she praying for, I wondered, Heaven, or everyone around her?

I wondered if I should increase my volume to compete with her.

"No," came the reply.

I asked, "Why don't you compete, Lord?"

***"With whom?"* He replied.**

This caused me to smile. The Holy Spirit never competes with Himself, any more than He interrupts Himself. For Him to compete with man would be ridiculous.

So, I waited patiently for this woman who was attempting to make up in zeal what she lacked in wisdom. In time, if she really wanted to learn, the Holy Spirit would instruct her how to work with Him.

He lets us have our own way until we finally want His way more than ours. Then He will flow in and around us with truth and power. Give Him the light switch of your will and He will flood your life with the knowledge and love of Jesus the love He has for you and others.

It is sad to see people compete in the Kingdom of God. I've done it myself. I remember one time early on when I prayed, "Holy Spirit please give me more of the anointing. I need more of the anointing."

His reply really surprised me. *"Why do you want it? And what will you do with it?"*

I felt embarrassed, like a child who had been caught with her hand in the cookie jar. Unsure of how to reply, I blurted out, "I don't know, but I've heard other people pray that way."

Gently but strongly He explained, *"Why don't you just ask Me to show you how to move in the anointing you already have?"*

I pondered His reply. I had heard others make this request hundreds of times. It had sounded so spiritual but now He was helping me see that it was not a request from my heart, and it was not led by the Spirit of God. It was a request from my soul, which wanted more power for its own sake.

When this realization dawned on me, I shuddered and then I changed my request. I prayed "Holy Spirit, show me how to move more in the anointing." He replied, *"First, move out of the way."*

I didn't have to ask Him what this meant. He wanted me to set aside my agenda and be willing to move in whatever direction He wanted me to go, regardless of where I might have wanted to go.

YIELDING TO THE HOLY SPIRIT

There is a choice that must be made. He wants us to yield—to be under His control, as He works through us and for us. A yielded vessel is the opposite of one that is rigid or stiff. He wants us to be submissive, compliant, and alive to what He is doing.

"If we live in the Spirit, let us also walk in the Spirit" (Gal. 5:25). Sometimes it seems we've gotten this verse backward: "If we live in our flesh, the Spirit will not walk in our flesh."

The Spirit of Truth never lies. He wants us to die to self, so we can live in the Spirit and allow Him to move through us in order to lift up Jesus.

He yields to man more than man yields to Him. The flesh (our wills) needs to be trained to move out of the way of the Spirit. How do we ever learn this very important truth? By spending more time in fellowship with Him, so we will recognize Him more readily and learn to yield to Him.

Too often we see man's power at many church services when we're starving to taste God's power. One time during a meeting, the Spirit of God was flowing through me—much too powerfully and beautifully for it to have anything to do with me. I saw people crying, laughing, and worshiping, shining brightly with God's presence.

I smiled. "Lord," I thought, "You are showing off! Why?"

"I want people to see the power of Heaven so they will believe Heaven is real and that I am alive and have power to prove it."

He brought the Kingdom of God to earth that night, so man would know He has made a way for us to enter into eternal life.

"For the Kingdom of God is not in word, but in power" (1 Cor. 4:20).

"But ye shall receive power after that the Holy Ghost is come upon you, and ye shall be witnesses unto me both in Jerusalem, and in all Judea, and in Samaria, and unto the uttermost part of the earth" (Act. 1:8).

Did you ever try to prove the Kingdom of God has come? You can't. But He can. The power of God wonderfully proves His Kingdom has come. He has declared for all to see that Heaven is real and hell is real, as well.

Many people today doubt there is a hell. They can decide it isn't real, but that doesn't change the reality of it. An army can invade a land whose inhabitants don't believe such an army exists. They wake up one morning and look out the window to see tanks in the streets. The army that didn't exist is out there now, and the war has been lost. At this point it's a little late to change one's mind about the reality of the army!

THE VICTORY IS YOURS

Sad to say, many Christians today are living in defeat, because they do not fully understand that the victory is ours in Christ Jesus. Our basic lack of understanding this simple but profound truth gives satan the opportunity to pursue us through the open doors of our unbelief. It's because their wills have not been set in cement in the Kingdom of God.

God wants to prove His existence and His love to all who are seeking Him in truth. That is why He encourages us in His Word, *"But if from thence thou shalt seek the LORD thy God, thou shalt find Him, if thou seek Him with all thy heart and with all thy soul"* (Deut 4:29). He wants to be found! Look at all the beauty and glory in the heavens and on the earth, even in the smile of a baby. Everything points to His majesty and His intelligent and loving design.

The greatest man or woman who ever walked the earth is merely a creature who was created by God. Man may choose to deny this fact, but this does not change its truth. God has given a spirit to each individual, so they can be born again. With this new spirit they come in line for a new inheritance. They are offered a high position, one of fellowship in the deepest and most intimate sense, with their kind and loving heavenly Father.

Before coming to Him we are fallen creatures, yet He has always made provision for man's deliverance, whether in ancient days, when He fought for His own, leading them out of Egypt, or later on the Cross at Calvary, when He fought for His people against all the dominions of hell and its demons. He has never lost His vision for mankind.

In the beginning He created mankind to be His family, and this goal has never left His heart. He has never rescinded His invitation to us. He has never once stopped offering community to those who believe on His Son, the Lord Jesus Christ. Patiently He waits upon our free will to see if we, too, want to live within His family and become a part of His ordained, eternal family.

Man's freedom to choose is a dangerous and risky gift, but it is also one of the greatest gifts God has ever given to man. No demon nor power on earth can separate us from the Kingdom of God, but our own free will can. Our free will contains within it the power, all by itself, to send its owner into eternal damnation or into eternal heavenly bliss.

God, in His infinite love and wisdom, forces Himself upon no one. He is like a loving father, hoping and longing, reaching out to a child, so he can offer the child His most precious gift. Our heavenly Father offers us the gift He has cherished from the foundation of the world—the broken body of His Son.

When a man or a woman reaches up, receives and embraces the disfigured body of Jesus on the cross, he or she begins to change into the image of God's Son. As people exercise their free will and identify with the broken body of Jesus as their own identity, God heals their brokenness, completes them, and fills them with glorified resurrection power.

As we've seen, our own power can never prove that the Kingdom of God has come. But the power of God, through the broken body of His Son coming alive in us and shining through us, does indeed prove that the King of Heaven has come to declare His Kingdom upon the earth.

Chapter 16

The Holy Spirit is a Seed-Bearing Spirit

Holding on by a Thread

It may seem as if we're holding on to life by a single slender thread. Yet, even that thread serves a purpose. Rope or twine would be too thick to hold a button onto a piece of clothing. To a coat, a button is important, and a very thin thread holds the button in place. It allows the button enough flexibility to fit in a button hole, closing the coat to keep us dry and warm, and adding beauty to the coat.

Sometimes the reality of life leaves us in shock. We have high expectations and are at times left in fear and discouragement, holding on with little or no strength like that little button, clinging by a single thread.

At such times we need to look up to our God and just let Him hold us. He will make something out of every season of our life if we let Him. The Psalmist wrote, *"I waited patiently for the Lord, and He inclined unto me and heard my cry. He brought me up also out of an horrible pit, out of the miry clay and set my feet upon a rock, and established my goings. And He hath put a new song in my mouth, even praise unto our God, many shall trust in the Lord"* (Ps. 40:1-3).

He *does* see and hear us when we are in travail, and in His timing He will meet every need we have. We must know the thread we are holding onto can be used to open the coat of love that God has for us. This love will be used to "button" us more securely to Him, and then we will live under the coat of His love. We will know His warmth and protection from the cold and experience His shelter from the rain storms that can quickly come and leave us feeling wet, very alone, full of fear, too hurt to cry out, and numb.

As we discussed earlier, the appearance of faith is when I appear to myself and others to be walking, talking, and acting in faith. To have real faith, however, is to have the King of kings and Lord of lords dwelling deep within my heart.

Why is He called faithful? Because He never runs out of faith. *"And I saw Heaven opened, and behold a white horse and he that sat upon him was called Faithful and True, and in my righteousness he doth judge and make war"* (Rev. 19:11).

We really do not know our own hearts. We may think we do, but as the Word says in Jeremiah, *"The heart is deceitful above all things and desperately wicked: who can know it? I the Lord search the heart, I try the reins, even give every man according to his ways, and according to the fruit of his doings"* (Jer.17: 9-10).

DEEPER FAITH FOR DARKER DAYS

Most of us in our daily walk of faith do fine as long as the days are fine. But there is a deeper walk of faith that is required when we walk through dark days. Sometimes the pain of life can be so overwhelming, you may feel you have lost your faith. A feeling which is far worse than feeling you have not found it. If you have something and lose it, you know what you have lost; if you never had it, you never will know what you lost.

Each person has times in the valley and times atop the mountains. Some valleys may not look as deep as yours or mine, but to the person in the valley, it is very deep indeed. What exactly is this kind of valley? Anything that has us bound and held down. As the judge said when he was asked to define pornography, "I know it when I see it." Similarly we know when we are in a valley.

We must be careful not to judge anyone who is in the valley. I can remember being on a mountaintop and thinking how clear it all seemed. I saw the light and wondered why others did not see it as plainly as I did. They couldn't see it because they were in the tree-filled-valley, but I was standing above the tree line.

Each tree in the valley is a cross that we suffer and die on. Why does this happen? So that when we leave the valley, we will no longer carry our cross alone, because we will have Someone else who has come alongside of us to help. He is always faithful, even when I am not, because He loves me far more then I could ever love Him. That is a truth that comes clear to us only after we've spent some time in the valley.

Jesus' own "valley of decision" was the Garden of Gethsemane the night before He was arrested. He prayed, *"O my Father, if the cup may not pass away from me, except I drink it, thy will be done"* (Matt. 26:42). He had a choice: either He could go forward in suffering and then death, or He could call on the aid of 12 legions of angels from His Father. Had He chosen to be delivered, we would never have known the choice of life He now holds out to all mankind.

GOD'S STEADFAST LOVE

I cannot fathom the full extent of His steadfast love, but the same steadfast love and mercy are new every morning for us. The Bible says, *"It is of the Lord's mercies that we are not consumed, because His compassions fail not. They are new every morning, great is thy faithfulness"* (Lam. 3:22-23). Daily He offers Himself to us! I cannot help but ponder the question: What is man that Jesus, the lover of our souls, would suffer and die, so we would belong to Him forever.

Divine ownership of my soul humbles me, yet at the same time, it comforts me. Jesus said, *"I am the Good Shepherd; I know My sheep, and My sheep know Me"* (John 10:14). This is a two-fold invitation: first, the Lord can know me; second, I can know Him.

The seed of eternal promise was placed in Mary's womb when the Holy Spirit came upon her. Mankind has been lost since Adam's fall, but the seed of promise was never lost. It proceeded, incorruptible, all the way to the cross and back up to Heaven.

Jesus is the only incorruptible seed the world has ever seen and will ever need. Why? Because He is the eternal seed of life. The Psalmist writes, *"As the father has compassion on his children, so the Lord has compassion on those who fear Him. For He knows how we are formed and remembers that we are dust. As for man, his days are like grass. He flourishes like a flower in the field. The wind blows over it, and it is gone and its place remembers it no more. But from everlasting to everlasting, the Lord's love is with those that fear Him and His righteousness with their children's children with those who keep His covenant and remember to obey His precepts, the Lord has established His throne in Heaven and His kingdom rules over all"* (Ps. 103:13-19).

He is *established*! We have a never changing King of kings, one who does not change upon popular demand! He prepared His own throne, and it stayed intact waiting for Him while He was on earth reaching out with love for all of us.

In my spirit, I can hear Jesus singing this song to us:

Love heals. Love sets free.

Love is the way to My kingdom, cries the man from Galilee.

Love is the gift I offer. Love is the life I give.

Love is the answer, no matter how you once lived.

I shall tell you the meaning so you can understand.

It is the love that draws you into My promised land.

This is the language that we speak.

This is My love that never knew defeat.

This love is higher than the earth,

but low enough to give new birth!

L is for living the life I bring. It grows in your heart until you want to sing.

O is an unbroken circle, no beginning and no end—like my love for you, my dear friend.

V is the voice of love that whispers to you of victory, when you grow weary.

E is the last letter in the word love. It stands for eternity; always living in my love.

FRUIT-BEARING SEEDS OF LIFE

The Holy Spirit is a seed-planting and a seed-bearing Spirit. His seeds, include dreams, destinies, callings, talents, and gifts He wants to water in your life. Have the seeds He has planted in your heart borne fruit that lifts up Jesus?

Our flesh (the soulish man, selfish ambition, competition, rebellion, etc.) can plant corruptible seeds that always lead to pain and death. The Holy Spirit knows what to allow in our lives in order to keep His seeds watered within us while they grow under the watchful eye of the Son.

Paul writes, *"But thanks be to God which giveth us the victory through our Lord Jesus Christ!"* (1 Cor. 15:57).

This victory verse is frequently sung and spoken, yet its real meaning comes only after we have fought the battle of faith and won! Some come marching out in full force, while others come limping and crawling out of the valley while still declaring that His goodness, faithfulness, grace, and mercy have brought them through.

Chapter 17

The Spirit of Circumferences

SAY NO TO FEAR

Life on earth gives us many chances for us to grow in the knowledge of who we are called to be. Each of these chances present us with a choice as to how we will respond. The Bible says, *"Because those who are led by the spirit of God are sons of God, for you did not receive a spirit that makes you a slave again to fear, but you received the spirit of sonship, and by Him we cry, "Abba, Father"* (Rom. 8:14-15). Our answer should be to say no to fear and yes to faith. And if our answer is no to fear, then we have just moved into the authority that has been given to us as children of God. We have also moved into agreement with the Word of God, which states in Second Timothy, *"For God hath not given us a spirit of fear, but of power, love and a sound mind"* (2 Tim. 1:7).

When we respond in faith, we are saying yes and amen and we are allowing faith to do the work that needs to be done. It tears down all forms of counterfeit faith, which can come to us in the form of fear. In so doing, we have moved out of agreement with fear. We break the old covenant with fear, and come into full agreement and full covenant with the spirit of faith, as a son and daughter of the Most High God.

THE HEART OF THE FATHER

The Spirit of God always leads us to the heart of the Father who loves us and the heart of Jesus who justified us with His blood for the total remission of all our sins. It is then that we receive divine adoption papers with our name written on them. We become heirs of God and joint heirs with Christ, so that if we suffer with Him, we may also be glorified with Him.

Jesus was called a man of sorrows. Our sorrows actually clothed Him when He was on the cross. When we go through grief and sorrow, it helps to remember that He has already been there before us. Even in our sorrows, we are still walking with Him and toward Him. If we had eyes to see in the Spirit realm, we would see that He carries us with all of our sorrows and pain. He wants to carry us, as a shepherd would carry a lamb in need of help.

There are many reasons why people do not trust the Lord. Some of these reasons are real, and some are placed in our hearts by fear! John writes *"There is no fear in love, but perfect love casteth out fear because fear hath torment. He that feareth is not made perfect in love. We love him because he first loved us"* (1 John 4:18-19).

When we realize that the One who first loved us has adopted us into His family, our fear dissipates. The Holy Spirit is the One who serves our "adoption papers" to us and then explains in detail what is written in them, so we will know what to do and say in every situation.

A Circle of Protection and Love

In a very real sense the Holy Spirit is the "Spirit of circumferences." He puts a full circle around the family of God. He encircles the Bride of Christ in order to mold and change her into who she is called to be.

Always remember the Bible was written under the inspiration of the Holy Spirit. He gave us this book of truth to live by. He came and is still here to reveal more and more truth to us.

The Holy Spirit longs for the Bride of Christ to grow up with a full understanding of who she is and who she is not. He wants her to know that the love of God is always for her and never against her.

Paul writes, *"Who shall separate us from the love of Christ? Shall tribulation, or distress, or peril, or sword? As it is written, For thy sake we are killed all day long. We are accounted as sheep for the slaughter. Nay, in all these things we are more than conquerors through Him that loved us. For I am persuaded, that neither death, nor life, nor angels, nor principalities, nor things to come, nor height, nor depth, nor any creation, shall be able to separate us from the love of God which is in Christ Jesus our Lord."* (Rom. 8:35-39).

CLEARING OUR UNDERSTANDING

God's Word is truth. It reveals God's love and thoughts to us. Many people struggle to comprehend the love of God. Because of this, fear may invade this place of "clouded understanding." This means we must clear our understanding by eradicating our fear in order to be free. How do we do this? By taking every lie and killing them with a truth—God's Word is a "love letter" of truth.

The Word of God is powerful enough to break down all lies while depositing living truth within us. *"Forever, O Lord, thy word is settled in Heaven"* (Ps. 119:89). God wants to assure us that He and His Word do not change according to our situations or feelings. He wants to enlighten our understanding, so we can know peace and joy.

It grieves the Holy Spirit when we move out of joy and give our peace away. It grieves Him to know that it is the devil who takes our peace. When fear reigns, peace and joy go into submission. They depart, leaving us feeling abandoned and weak. At such times, fear takes its foothold and makes us feel defeated.

We read. *"The entrance of thy words giveth light. It giveth understanding unto the simple"* (Ps. 119:130). When we receive a greater level of understanding from God's Word, we can walk in greater freedom. For a person to be truly free, he must have a spirit that is free, one that dominates both flesh and soul. This is hard to grasp, because we dwell in a world of seeing, feelings, and doing. But God asks us to dwell in the spiritual realm, under the control of His Holy Spirit, filled with the pure wisdom of God's Word of truth.

SPIRITUAL TRUTH

Our soul may be too attached to this world to be able to receive the deeper levels of truth, but our "spirit man" can receive and enter into these realms, for the truth is available to all. The Bible says *"Which things also we speak, not in the words which man's wisdom teacheth, but which the Holy Ghost teacheth; comparing spiritual things with spiritual"* (1 Cor. 2:13).

Are you hungry for a spiritual understanding of the deeper truths of God that are buried like diamonds in a mine? Do you desire to search out heavenly treasures of wisdom that are within the Holy Spirit's understanding? If you do, pray the following prayer for greater wisdom and revelation.

A PERSONAL PRAYER

Precious Holy Spirit, I ask that you would provide me with a greater level of understanding of my destiny, that I would always remember that the Father created me to walk in His Truth. I ask for pure wisdom, so I can grasp the mind of Christ and have a deeper revelation of the treasures that are hidden in the Word of God.

I ask you to help me discern and understand the greater truths, so I can have freedom and walk hand in hand with my Good Shepherd, and so I can place my other hand in the hand of my loving Father.

Father, I have a desire in my heart to cry out, "Abba, Father" because my heart is full of love. Bring me into communion with You and Your love. Change my world and let me experience Your world. Bring me out of my soulish realm and let me enter a greater spiritual realm under the control of the Holy Spirit for I want to lift up Jesus.

Holy Spirit, become "the spirit of circumference" around my family and all those I love. Help us to understand who we were created to be so Jesus would be glorified. Amen.

Chapter 18

The Holy Spirit Understands All

AN ABIDING ANOINTING

The Holy Spirit can impart understanding to our spirits, because He understands all things. *"But ye have an unction from the Holy One, and ye know all things."* (1 John 2:20). 'Unction' means the act of anointing as a rite of consecration or healing. *"But the anointing which ye have received of him abideth in you, and ye need not that any man teach you, but as the same anointing teacheth you all things, and is truth, and is no lie and ever as it hath taught you, ye shall abide in him"* (1 John 2:27).

The anointing is the key that opens our understanding. We must receive the anointing from Him. Just as we have a choice to accept and receive the Holy Spirit into these "temples" (our bodies), so we have a choice to accept the anointing.

God is looking for willing recipients. How open we are to receive will determine how much we will be able to contain. The choice of how open we are is up to us.

The word "receive" has many wonderful meanings:

1. To take in or accept (as something sent or paid). (Does this remind you of your acceptance of the gift of your salvation?)

2. To come into possession of, get hold, or contain.

3. To permit to enter, greet, or welcome. (This sounds like a heart issue, and a willingness to go beyond our normal trust level or human understanding.)

4. To be a home to visitors.

5. To accept as true or authoritative.

6. To be the subject of or undergo experience.

7. To change incoming radio waves into sound or pictures. (That sounds like the spreading of the gospel; a going forth and declaring what God has done for me and then telling others what He can do for them.)

OPEN THE LINES OF COMMUNICATION

If the telephone receiver is on the phone, it will not do you any good, even if you yell at it. You must choose to act by picking up the receiver and holding it to your mouth and ear. No matter how desperate you are to talk or hear someone, in order to make the receiver work, you must first pick it up.

Many people have hung up on God or left the receiver off the hook because they feel they have no need to hear from or speak to Him. Many times the phone lines seem dead to us and we do not feel connected. These dead lines happen at different times in our lives, but when they do, we often feel that God is silent. We long to hear His voice, but it is simply a matter of reconnecting our hearts to His heart, putting our heart back into the position of being "hooked" on Him, so the phone lines that once were dead will come back to life again. When this happens we have become reconnected.

Part of the work Jesus did on the cross was to become a "telephone line man," laying bloodlines so we can go freely to the throne of grace. The Bible says, *"Seeing then that we have a great high priest, that is passed unto heavens, Jesus the Son of God, let us hold fast our profession. For we have not an high priest which cannot be touched with the feeling of our infirmities, but was in all points tempted like as we are, yet without sin. Let us therefore come boldly unto the throne of grace, that we may obtain mercy and find grace to help in time of need"* (Heb 4:14-16).

Jesus laid His bloodlines with the great hope that we would, could, and should use them at all times. However, we must become vulnerable, and this puts us in a position of risking being hurt. At the same time, it puts us in a position to be healed as a result of staying open.

The Holy Spirit wants to show us the bloodlines Christ has laid so we can hook into them and receive from Heaven. He wants to plug in the anointing for us and in us so we will always be connected to our heavenly Father and Jesus. The Holy Spirit is like the "line inspector" who sees weak areas that need to be strengthened so they can function and perform well.

It is He who points you to the One who strengthens you—Jesus! Peter writes, *"But the God of all grace who hath called us unto his eternal glory by Christ Jesus, after that ye have suffered a little while, make you perfect, establish, strengthen, settle you"* (1 Peter 5:10).

I would ask you right now to look into your own heart with all truth and examine it to see if your "phone is on the hook," and to discover if there is any interference on the phone lines in the form of sin, disobedience, unbelief, anger, or fear. Ask God right now for forgiveness and ask the Holy Spirit to show you clearly if there are any weaknesses in your phone line connection that need to be repaired.

The God of all grace has put in a call to us. Are you there to take the call? If the answer is no, then ask Him now to remove and heal all blockages, crossed wires and short-circuits on the line.

Now, with His strength and His grace, be willing to reach out again and let the power of His Spirit fill your mind and heart with the peace that surpasses all understanding, so you can receive His call and respond with a sound mind and an undivided heart.

A TRUSTING HEART

When we're fairly certain good and wonderful things will happen to us, it is easy to stay entirely open. The reason so many fear becoming vulnerable stems from their fear of the unknown and uncomfortable situations. There is only one way to break away from these fears, and that is by knowing the heart of the Person to whom you have yielded your will.

Have you ever sat in an airplane, realizing the pilot has control of your life and safety? He or she is usually a total stranger, yet you probably place blind faith in him or her, because of training and the safety record of the airline company. Usually we do not question the pilot's credentials, because we feel it would embarrass and humiliate him or her, and we have no right to do so. Yet, we may do this daily to God through unbelief, as if we were demanding to see His credentials.

If we were to reject the pilot for lack of trust, we could never fly —at least, not with that particular pilot. Believe me the Holy Spirit understands rejection. Millions reject Him every day. Jesus told us to receive Him, yet many reject him with both words and actions.

The Holy Spirit understands that fear and indifference are the main ingredients of rejection. Usually the fear of losing control of something or someone becomes a major block to our ability to trust. Jesus had complete faith in His Father, as He cried out from the cross. He trusted His Father's heart of love for He knew His Father would always be faithful to Him.

Jesus was held on the cross by a thread of faith, and this was more than enough. And from this thread, our robes of righteousness were woven. The color of the thread was blood-red for it came from the Savior's death. Then changed to white, when He rose from the dead and put on us the white robes of His righteousness that He alone could place on us now and forever.

Paul writes, *"But of him are ye in Christ Jesus, who of God is made unto us wisdom and righteousness, and sanctification, and redemption"* (1 Cor. 1:30).

PERSONAL APPLICATION

Here are some heart-searching questions: Is there a special area in your life in which you feel you are hanging on by a thin thread of hope?

Will you ask Jesus to wrap the thread of hope around His heart so He can bring healing to your heart?

Have you "hung up" on God, because of fear or pain?

Do you want the Holy Spirit to search the lines of heavenly connection and reconnect you for full service again?

Are you willing to let go of all fears that hold you back from the presence of God? If so, then pray the following prayer.

A PERSONAL PRAYER

Father help me in all areas of my life. Take every fear from me. Remove fears of the known and the unknown from my heart. I ask for a free spirit, so I will be able to follow the Holy Spirit, as He leads me from glory to glory in Christ Jesus.

Remove all barriers I have put up or ones that life has placed upon me that block my relationship with you from growing deeper and closer. I give you my will, and I ask you to reveal your will to me. I choose to be a receiver for you. So Father, I yield myself totally to you. Help me to be more vulnerable and open to you and to others so the Kingdom of God will be able to flow out of me more and more.

Holy Spirit, flow out of me freely and lift up Jesus in a greater way in me and through me.

Thank you, Father, for the love you have shed abroad in my heart and over my life and upon those I love. I am yours forever. Amen.

As you have called out to God, He is calling back to you. This is what He wants you to understand.

He called them all, each one by name.

This is the reason that He came.

But some grew proud and pulled away.

Others too went astray.

They turned so far, they lost their sight.

They cried out, "Is this life?"

They fell deeper, also others went.

They were all lost, and none could be sent.

They could no longer hear and no longer see,

but God's pure love followed after thee.

He never once left from their side,

but He was no longer allowed to be their Guide.

So many said, "I'll show you the way,"

but they themselves had gone astray.

They placed burdens on those who followed,

but the love they offered was soon shown as hollow.

Then God in His mercy cried out to man,

"Come to Me. I have a plan.

I'll give you My Son.

I'll make Him like you,

my love, and hope He'll carry to you."

So with arms of love and a heart full of hope,

these are the words that He spoke.

"They shall see, and return to Me."

For none shall be lost, I'll set them free.

So, He was born just as a man,

but within Him a new life began.

Many followed and He showed them the way,

but others refused and continued to stray.

For those who followed, He now called them son,

and in their hearts the new life did come.

He cried out again, and this they heard.

"I saw you arise and hoped you would call.

I gently carried you, when I saw you fall

for I have a plan that will bring you life.

Life that is full, one we will share."

I would speak to you of love.

and share Myself with you.

Never leaving you alone,

for I would always be true.

True through your doubts. True through your tears.

Always with you, for all eternal years.

for you are Mine and Mine alone.

Will you come and rest by My throne?

Please come, My beloved. Sit by My side.

I long to lead you and be your Guide.

I call you holy. I call you true,

for with each step I draw closer to you.

Now we are one in the Spirit,

Truth has set you free.

None other can have you, for you belong to Me.

For My love is upon you and also will be

Your Guide.

Chapter 19

The Breath of God

SURRENDER TO GRACE

Ignorance is a powerful weapon, especially when someone uses a person's ignorance to make him/her bound and trapped. Why are so many of God's children just barely making it through life while white-knuckled fear seems to have so much power over their lives?

It may simply be that they have not accepted their new position in Jesus! *"Therefore if any man be in Christ, he is a new creature. Old things are passed away; behold, all things are become new"* (2 Cor. 5:17).

It is easy to sit in church and say amen to a preacher's words, but to sit in Christ Jesus and understand what it means to carry the authority of a believer, is a challenging process. You can only walk in what you know. You can only feel peace if you dwell in truth and hope.

Paul greeted the Ephesians with these words: *"Grace be to you and peace from God our Father and from the Lord Jesus Christ"* (Eph. 1:2). Paul understood what it meant to be positioned in Christ. And we must go back to an elementary understanding of the gift of God's grace and love toward us. Indeed, we must surrender to the grace that God offers us daily.

Do we really understand the depth of "peace from God our Father and from the Lord Jesus Christ"? Many of us are still wrestling with God, hoping we can win Him over, so we can finally have peace with Him. But God wants us to experience "His peace within us." Then we can walk in truth.

If we truly understood His goodness, grace, and mercy toward us, we would find that all of life would be different for us. This is a privilege that is offered to all mankind. As John states so clearly, *"For God so loved the world that he gave his only begotten son, that whosoever believeth in Him should not perish but have everlasting life"* (John 3:16).

Not only are we called to *believe in* Jesus, but we're called to *be in* Him, both now and forever. Paul writes, *"For by grace are ye saved through faith and that not of yourselves; it is a gift of God, not of works, lest any man should boast for we are his workmanship created in Christ Jesus unto good works, which God hath ordained that we should walk in"* (Eph. 2:8-10).

God has ordained certain works for us to walk in; not in ourselves, our mind, our will and our emotion, but only in Christ Jesus. He wants us to know the mind of Christ, not the mind of the world.

The following verse illustrates this truth for us: *"But God who is rich in mercy for His great love wherewith He loved us. Even when we were dead in sin, hath quickened us together with Christ* (by grace we are saved) *and hath raised us up together and made us sit together in heavenly places in Christ Jesus that in the ages to come he might show the exceeding riches of his grace in his kindness toward us through Christ Jesus"* (Eph. 2:4-7). God wants this message of truth to ring in our hearts. In the same way that a message of love can come through a song or a letter, God sent a message of love to us through Jesus.

When Jesus died, the severe wounds in His body broadcasted for the love of God to the world. We need only to listen and keep on listening to that message. The Holy Spirit loves to teach us about the Cross of Jesus Christ and the love of God. The blood of Jesus opens the door to the presence of the Holy Spirit. Such love and loyalty are not common on earth, yet God wants to have that same kind of fellowship with us that Jesus had with the Holy Spirit.

God the Father wants us to function with Jesus' faith, love, humility, mind, life, and spirit, but this can only be accomplished *with* Him, and *through* Him. The Holy Spirit recognizes only one Savior. He is the Spirit of Truth, and as such He places all glory where it belongs. He is to the living Word of God, Jesus, and to His written Word as well.

GOD'S PERFECT LOVE

John explains the Trinity as follows: *"For there are three that bear record in Heaven, the Father, the Word and the Holy Ghost; and these three are one"* (1 John 5:7). They are one and they always were and will be one, and they want us to become "one in Christ Jesus." Jesus prayed, *"My prayer is not for them alone. I pray also for those who will believe in Me through their message. That all of them may be one. Father, just as You are in Me and I am in You, may they also be in Us, so that the world may believe that You have sent me. I have given them the glory that you have gave Me, that they may be one, as We are one…"* (John 17:20-22 NIV).

Nature provides us with many illustrations that help us understand the Trinity. One beautiful symbol is a thunderstorm. Let us imagine the Father as the thunder that speaks during a storm; His son Jesus is the lightning and when lightning strikes things always change. Jesus is the Light of the World. There is a sense in which the rain is the Holy Spirit. Like the rain He falls all around us, causing us to be refreshed so we can grow into our highest calling.

Yes God has given us many reminders of His perfect love toward us. Is your spirit open enough to see them? A thunderstorm brings both terror and fear, but it is also a reminder of the faithful love of the Godhead. Some storms leave great devastation in their wake. Others revive drought-wilted crops and freshen the air, restoring hope and expectation. How we choose to respond to God during the storms of our life, will bring either positive or negative results. The choice is ours. We can fight God and lose or we can flow with Him, knowing He is always "fighting" for us.

The Godhead wants the Bride to be positioned in Christ Jesus, full of joy, peace, and hope. Few men, waiting at the altar for the woman they are going to marry, want her to arrive at the alter looking disheveled and beaten up. Yet some Christians are beaten down by sad teachings that hold them down, bound to their groom in fear, not bound together by love. God's perfect love casts out all fear.

The Groom wants to lavish a pure powerful and jealous love upon his Bride. That is what Christ Jesus wants to do for you. He wants us to become His beaming Bride, filled with joy and strength. He is looking for a Bride who shows the world that He is a heavenly bridegroom. He wants a Bride who reflects a heavenly vision. As stated before, a beaten-up, battered, despairing, and confused Bride leaves the impression that Jesus is a "wife abuser."

As His bride, what kind of reflection do other people see? Do you look like someone who has been abused by your spouse? Or do you come across as one who is deeply loved and cherished? Do you doubt Jesus' love for you? He laid His life down for you, in the greatest act of eternal commitment the world has ever seen.

The Spirit of God wants to breathe *life*, not spiritual death, into the Bride of Christ. He wants to breathe into her the new resurrected life that Jesus purchased for her. Will we open our mouths and allow Him to do so or will we push away the One who carries the breath of God?

We may never admit that we lack confidence in the Holy Spirit, but maybe we are showing it. We schedule meetings that we have planned so tightly that the agenda is laid in solid concrete and we refuse to alter our plans one iota. In order for the Holy Spirit to breathe life into someone or something, they must be willing to let Him do so.

When the Holy Spirit does breathe on someone or something, you can usually sense the touch of eternity. The breath of God is from an eternal kingdom that has no end; when He breathes on something, it becomes part of His eternal creation.

Just as our earthly bodies need oxygen to survive, our spirits need the breath of God to come alive and stay alive. The breath of God caused man to become a living spirit, and it may be that in this way He was setting a pattern for us to follow—a way of life. He wanted us to realize how vital it is, that the breath of God has blown on our work before we move ahead.

The Book of Acts describes a man named Cornelius who was seeking to know the will and ways of God: *"Four days ago I was fasting until this hour, and at the ninth hour I prayed in my house, and behold, a man stood before me in bright clothes and said, 'Cornelius, thy prayer is heard and thine alms are had in remembrance in the sight of God. Send, therefore, to Joppa and call hither Simon, whose surname is Peter. He is lodged in one Simeon, a tanner, by the seaside who when he cometh shall speak unto thee"* (Acts 10:30-33).

Through prayer and fasting, Cornelius was opening himself up to hear from God. Not only was a message going to be given to him and to those he loved, but his life and the lives of those he loved would be changed forever.

Cornelius was focusing on what was going on in the spiritual realm. The clarity of how God led Cornelius was wonderful, and so were the precise instructions that God gave to him. Like so many of us, Cornelius had to get over his fear, in order to be able to listen and to be able to speak. *"And when he looked on him, he was afraid, and said, What is it, Lord?"*(Acts 10:4).

Cornelius then received divine directions with specific confirming details. He was told everything he needed to know: the time and place, and who and how many were going to be sent to him, and whence they had come from. Obviously, he was totally open to the vision and instruction of the Holy Spirit. He wanted details, and he got them.

Most important of all, he followed the directions he'd been given with instant and meticulous obedience. He did not delay modify, or "improve" on them, and he did not lean on the strength of his own intellect. He simply did exactly what he was told to do.

He was told to call for Peter by sending men to him. How many times have I not been able to receive such clear directions because of lack of prayer and fasting in my life. Had I been in Cornelius's place, I probably would have put it off until I had done other things—good things, godly things—that I felt I had to do, and then I would have gone myself, to make sure it was done right.

Not so with Cornelius. He was wise enough and yielded enough to follow directions. He sent two servants after telling them all the things he had learned. What do you suppose they talked about as they traveled to Joppa? Did they think their master was losing his mind? Was he being too heavenly minded to be any earthly good?

They knew him well, as did the third man who went with them—a devout soldier. These men must have had a faithful track record, for Cornelius entrusted such a critical assignment into their hands.

Meanwhile, on a housetop in Joppa, Peter was praying. Intense spiritual activity can build quite an appetite, and Peter was hungry. In fact he was ravenous. He could probably smell the bread baking and the roast of lamb turning on the spit. Even so he chose not to eat. I've done that, especially when I've been ministering. I believe we can receive from God better on an empty stomach than we can after we eat.

So Peter chose not to eat and he fell into a trance. He gave up food and saw Heaven open. Then he had a heavenly vision that would forever change the way the Gospel of Jesus Christ was spread around the world.

What a loving God we serve! His timing is always perfect. But what about our obedience? How many times have we missed an open Heaven, because of our disobedience?

Chapter 20

The Production

THE VISION

Let's consider Peter's experience as a dramatic production entitled, "The Vision." The Holy Spirit was setting the stage—a rooftop at least—so He could put on this production (Acts 10, 11:12). The production would involve a four-corner sheet being let down from Heaven to the earth. It would also have included different kinds of four-footed beasts, plus creeping things and birds of the air. They were all alive, so they were probably making quite a racket, moving, stretching, and jumping around!

After viewing this "production," Peter was told, *"Rise, kill, and eat."* Lacking a full understanding of the vision, he refused. After all there were animals with cloven hooves on that sheet! While he was pondering this, the Holy Spirit said, *"Behold, three men seek thee."*

Are we like Peter, demanding that we understand everything before we will obey? The great news is that when the Holy Spirit switches on the light of our understanding, we finally get the meaning, because the spirit of man is always taught by the Spirit of God.

Had Peter remained in his own limited understanding that was based on the traditions of man, he would probably still be arguing with "The Vision," but the Holy Spirit drew him away by telling him of the three men who had come to see him.

Of course, when Peter descended from the rooftop, there they were just as the Holy Spirit had said they would be. That incredible confirmation that He was hearing God accurately did much to change his mind about the meaning of the vision, and God's command to kill and eat.

Many years ago, I was asked to teach at a "Life in the Spirit" seminar. I had been born again barely three months earlier, so I felt woefully inadequate to do so. But the other people had prayed, and God had given them my name as being the one who was to teach them on the topic of God's love.

I did not want to be in front of people. On the contrary, I was having a wonderful time alone with the Lord in praise, prayer, and worship. Actually, I had no idea of what to do, but I did trust their ability to hear God.

What was I going to do? I wanted to please God with my whole heart, yet fear was knocking at my door, and I was answering it! Moreover, I agreed with the fear, which said I had no training, was not a known Bible teacher, and did not even like to talk in front of people.

As I got serious about praying about this, however, I felt I needed to go on a "Daniel fast." Like that Old Testament prophet, I surely needed the wisdom of God. *"Prove thy servants, I beseech thee, ten days and let them give us pulse to eat and water to drink"* (Dan. 1:12). The only pulse I knew of at that time was the one that came from my heartbeat.

Before I could obey my leading and begin the fast, I knew I'd better find out what this 'pulse' Daniel referred to was. It didn't take me long to learn what it meant. It was fruit and vegetables. Well, I reasoned I can handle that! Ten days? No problem! With breathtaking zeal I gave up all other food and with my tummy full of vegetables I began praying for God to show me what to teach and how to teach it.

Listening to the Holy Spirit

Even so, I soon grew frustrated. It seemed certain that God would speak all right, but *not* about the subject I wanted to hear about! Seemingly pleased that I was at last sitting still and concentrating on what

He might say to me, He took the opportunity to tell me many things but none of what He told me dealt with my assigned subject.

I reasoned that I would have to do it without Him. As I was preparing my talk, I arranged to go over to the house of my friend, Irene, to pray and study. Running a little late, I had not had time to eat before I left. As I turned into her street, the Holy Spirit spoke to me. *"Ask her for some homemade vegetable soup to eat, for she has just made some."*

I was new at hearing the Holy Spirit, but I knew it was Him. Therefore when I arrived at Irene's front door I said, "The Holy Spirit just told me to ask you for some homemade vegetable soup that you have in your refrigerator and have just made."

Irene stared at me, her eyes grew wide with amazement. She replied, "I don't know if I like the Lord knowing I just put some fresh vegetable soup in my refrigerator, but I'll heat it up for you."

It was a "goose-bump moment" for both of us. He was training me to listen to small details that would confirm what I was hearing. Next He said, *"I want you to learn to recognize my voice, so when I tell you something, you will know it is Me."* He was actually training me to flow in the gifts of the Holy Spirit!

At times I have misunderstood and have not recognized His voice, just as I've missed or not understood my husband, Fred, whose voice I've heard thousands of times in our 40 years of marriage. I'd learned to listen carefully for Fred; now I was learning to listen carefully for the voice of the Holy Spirit.

Some people who *could* hear Him are afraid of not hearing Him accurately, So they turn their listening ears off rather than take the risk of turning them on. After many years, I've come to realize that my part is *to be willing to listen,* and His part is *to speak in such a way that I will hear.* I therefore always pray for a listening ear. I want one ear to be turned to Heaven and the other turned to earth.

There's always something going on in the spiritual realm, but if we've been too busy or full of other things to listen, then we'll not be able to tune into it. This doesn't mean nothing's going on; it just means we've become too busy to hear it, and/or we've tuned it out.

Sometimes the Holy Spirit speaks in a small breeze; at other times He speaks like a mighty, rushing wind. It's not important how He speaks; it's whether we have a listening ear. The Spirit of the Lord is calling out to a people who will recognize His breath, as it caresses their cheek and wafts around their listening ears. Sensing His presence, they will concentrate on the breathing of His words as He breathes revelation on them regarding what is occurring in the spiritual realm.

To recognize the breath of God, you must be close enough to feel it. He offers you this gift, but, as always, it is up to us, whether we will be open enough to receive it. The Holy Spirit longs to breathe on the Bride of Christ. He longs to help carry her sorrows and pain, and He longs to whisper His words of comfort and love to her.

Even Job needed this. He said, *"The Spirit of God hath made me, and the breath of the almighty hath given me life"* (Job 33:4). I love that verse and all that it implies! It is describing one of the truths that will come to us after a season of testing or during a time of affliction, at a time when we may have been struggling and trying to hear the voice of the Lord. It is during such times that the Lord will breathe life into us, through words of encouragement, hope, and instruction.

Sometimes it comes when a person has been given revelation knowledge, but they may feel they have nothing left within. In their absolute emptiness, they long for the breath of God and begin to realize that all they have left is the breath of God. At such a time, you may hear them sing a song, such as this one that has been sung by believers for ages.

"I look up from under the burdens that I carry. I feel so weak. I feel so weary. I tried to cry out, 'Oh, please! Come help me! I feel so lost. I feel so lonely.' Who has placed these weights upon me? Was it myself or from another? What difference does it make? I know now that they are mine and belong not to others.

"I started to walk but only to fall. I needed your help to lift them all. I sought help from others, but they, too, were weighed down by their burdens they carry. They, too, have fallen and are now left weary. I listen in the stillness; I hear men stumbling about. They too are seeking to find a way out.

"Who will carry our burdens? They have pulled us way down. We know that we are falling—is there no hope? My heart is full of sorrow. My eyes are full of tears. There is no answer for all the lost down here.

"There! Over there is one who can stand. I shall follow him. I will walk behind him and take hold of his hand. But the world has come upon him, and now I see that he, too, is lost—a broken man like me. We both have fallen under the cares of this life.

"We both had such hope and promise, but then we tasted life. It has left us empty and searching inside. But we will walk together and hope to find a guide. Yet—I feel so alone, with such a searching inside.

"He tells me of a Friend, who did not pass him by. This friend is Jesus, who speaks of love. He says He'll be our guide. As He looks in our eyes, He says to each of us,

"Come, follow Me.

I alone give life

now and for all eternity."

"Come, my friends,

won't you follow me?

I know the way,

and I shall set you free."

"All you will ever need

is found inside Me."

Chapter 21

Fine Tuning Your Hearing

SPIRITUAL UNDERSTANDING

If you were on a tour in a foreign country and your guide suddenly lost his voice, you might be looking at a great work of art or a city or place of historic interest and never know it nor know what it was.

Some years ago I was in Israel with a tour group when that actually happened to our guide. He lost his voice and was unable to explain the pivotal events that had taken place at the very spot on which we were standing. At the Sea of Galilee, we could see the water and we even took a boat ride across it. But it had far greater impact for us when a minister who was on tour with us opened his Bible and read what Jesus did there. It worked so well, in fact, that he kept doing this at each site we visited.

This is what the Holy Spirit wants to do for each of us today. He wants to accompany us to every spot so He can explain things to us and give us spiritual understanding. Sometimes He deposits an impression within us that stays with us forever. At other times His voice comes via environmental circumstances. He wants us to be able to hear Him in different ways and tones that are both soft and loud.

The Holy Spirit sets up stages around us, just as He did for Peter in "The Vision." Sometimes He uses people and situations to guide us—these are not always enjoyable moments. But when it comes to spreading the good news about Jesus, He takes His job very seriously and He expects us to do the same, for He is a very determined guide.

One time, as I was learning to fine tune my ability to hear the Holy Spirit He said to me, *"I want you to sell your vehicle and pay off all your bills and buy a house."*

In my mind I felt that there was no way that was God. For I thought at the time; we had just gotten that truck! And I was the one who picked it out! I said to myself, This will never witness to Fred. He'll say it's not God, and we'll get to keep my little "creampuff."

But when I told Fred about what I "thought" I'd heard the Holy Spirit say to me he nodded and to my surprise he said, "I've never really liked that truck."

We put an ad in the paper and waited. And waited. Not one call came about the vehicle. I thought, "Oops, I guess I didn't hear Him right, after all."

At the time, I was involved with our church's youth group and I had offered to drive some of the youth to a retreat, so off we went. After the retreat I returned my young passengers to their homes and I finally returned to mine.

It was the last day the newspaper ad would be running and there in front of our house, sat "Creampuff," an unpleasant reminder that I'd not heard the Holy Spirit or so I thought. About an hour after I got home however, a couple came by, gave Creampuff a test drive, and bought her on the spot. As a result my faith began to grow again, because I realized I had heard the voice of the Holy Spirit.

With the money we received for the truck we paid off our bills, but we still lacked transportation. We looked for another car, but if we bought the one we wanted, we would have gone back into debt.

Finally, we did find a car, but buying it would use up some of the money we would need for a down payment on our first house. We sighed and prayed and searched through the paper one more time. This time we found a car that we could afford and still have enough left over for the down payment. To our surprise, it was the same year, color, and model of the one we had wanted. The Holy Spirit was again confirming what He had spoken to me.

Next we began to look for a house, and we finally found the perfect one for us. We bought it and moved in. All seemed to go smoothly until six months later, when Fred came home and said, "Guess what? I've just received orders posting me to Germany for three years!"

I was stunned, actually I was in shock. "Lord," I prayed—or rather, demanded—"why did You do this now? What will we do with this house that you had us get?"

We belonged to a prayer group, and as we sat in the prayer meeting that night, the Holy Spirit said to me, *"Tell that couple you have a four-bedroom house for rent. They need it."*

I did exactly as He directed, and they were thrilled! We were thrilled as well.

I hate change and really hate being uprooted and transplanted. To cheer me up the Holy Spirit revealed His sense of humor to me. When Fred received the paperwork from his new company in Germany, their motto was emblazoned on their letterhead: "All the way by God." I laughed, in spite of myself.

And there was a nice P.S. to the house story. Not only did the renting family have the bigger house they needed while we were gone, when it came time to sell the house seven years later, it had doubled in value!

Look at the loving care of the Holy Spirit. He knew the family that would have need of the house and He knew its value would keep going up. (We had never even given this a thought.) I wonder if Peter would have given the Gentiles so much thought in the plan of salvation, if he had not received the spiritual vision that was accompanied by the Spirit's confirmation. His obedience to the heavenly vision opened the door to the entire world that the Gospel of Jesus Christ would be preached everywhere to Jews and Gentile alike.

Three men had sought out Peter to explain what Jesus did just as three wise men had sought out a babe in a manger. Both of these trios wanted to see what God was about to do. The Lord seems particularly fond of groups of three—perhaps because He is a member of the Trinity.

THE BREATH OF GOD

Cornelius was a wise man who stayed open to the plan of God. He wanted to make sure he did not miss out on what God was doing. The breath of God was blowing on the Day of Pentecost. And it is still blowing today.

Peter came to him and explained what was "blowing in the wind." The Spirit of God is still "blowing" the message of God's love around the world. He is still "blowing" on the work of salvation to keep Jesus lifted up throughout the earth. The Holy Spirit blows His supernatural breath that breathes supernatural life—the life of eternal salvation.

Our breath is limited, and so is the work we can do. We need the breath of God to blow loud and strong for all the world to see. We need to inhale His breath by becoming "breathing Christians"—who breathe in the breath of God. When we exhale, His breath comes out and changes the world. We are called to breathe over the areas where sin has brought death and destruction. Let us breathe the spirit of life wherever there is pain and death!

How do we do this?

First, we must pray for the Holy Spirit to flow through us.

Second, we must find a place of silence where we can hear what the Holy Spirit wants to breathe on and through us. We can only exhale, what we have inhaled.

Third, we must stay open to the Holy Spirit's plan and be willing to obey Him without needing to know why He wants us to do certain things.

Fourth, we must arrive at the same wisdom Gamaliel had when he addressed the Sanhedrin. *"And now I say unto you, refrain from these men, and let them alone: for if this counsel or this work be of men it will come to naught: But if it be of God, ye cannot overthrow it; lest haply ye be found even to fight against God"* (Acts 5:38-39).

PERSONAL APPLICATION

You can tell if *you* are fighting against God, by asking yourself these questions:

1. Am I really sure, deep inside my spirit, that I know the mind of Christ in this matter?

2. Have I prayed enough, or do I need to fast and pray more so I can get the release in my spirit that this is the timing and will of God for me now?

3. Do I have the peace of God so I can be led in peace and not fear?

4. Do I feel led or do I feel driven?

5. Has the Holy Spirit within me given my spirit a witness of agreement so I am not struggling against but flowing in the will of God?

A PERSONAL PRAYER

Let us pray now, and ask the Holy Spirit to breathe on us:

Dear Holy Spirit, I again ask You for the gift of trust that is like the trust You and Jesus share. I ask You to please breathe upon me and through me. Empower me afresh. Lead me to the places and people You have called and planned for me to be a part of. Allow me to have an ear to hear what You are speaking. Help me to be always on a rooftop like Peter, with an open, hungry heart. I ask that You be my personal Guide and explain to me all I need to know in order to work with You and through You so I can lift up Jesus in my life. I love You and thank You, my faithful collaborator. I need You and want You, now and always. Amen.

Paul writes, *"But it is written, eyes have not seen, nor ears heard, neither hath entered into the heart of man, the things which God hath prepared for them that love Him. But God hath revealed them unto us by His Spirit, for the spirit searcheth all things, yea, the deep things of God"* (1Cor. 2:9-10).

Do you really love Him? Do you really want the deep things of God? If you do, then this is a promise from the Word to you. God longs to reveal things to you by His spirit. The small word 'by' makes us think we must be by (or next to) His Spirit, in order for Him to reveal what God has prepared for us.

The Holy Spirit loves to reveal more light to you with regard to the person of Jesus, the Father, and the Word of God. That is why He is called the Spirit of Enlightenment. He wants us to be so close to Him that when He whispers in our ears, our eyes will be opened, and new Kingdom truths will enter into our hearts.

Chapter 22

Spirit of Enlightenment

The Spirit's Heart

One of my favorite events in Jesus' life was when He stood up in the Temple and read the following words from the book of Isaiah: *"The Spirit of the Lord is upon me, because he hath anointed me to preach the gospel to the poor; he hath sent me to heal the brokenhearted, to preach deliverance to the captives, and recovering of sight to the blind, to set at liberty them that are bruised, To preach the acceptable year of the Lord"* (Luke 4:18-19).

Many churches today seem to have received this message in their heads, but not in their hearts and spirits. The same Spirit carries the same message today and forever. He wants to preach the good news, not to give a dry history lesson. He wants to proclaim His story, not history. He wants to proclaim, farther and wider than ever before, the news of the greatest proclamation ever made.

What is in the heart of the Spirit regarding this? He has a burning desire to make every follower and true believer into a *proclaimer*. As they claim things for the Kingdom of God, they bring glory to the name of Jesus. As they walk in that role, they themselves will be blessed and will be able to release blessings upon others.

He trains them to be proclaimers, wanting each one to come into a true understanding of the things God has prepared for them, now and forever, so they can proclaim these things to others.

Remember when the Holy Spirit was first spoken of in the very first verse in the Bible? *"In the beginning God created the heaven and the earth. The earth was without form and void, and darkness was upon the face of the deep, and the Spirit of God moved upon the face of the waters, and God said, let there be light, and there was light"* (Gen. 1:1-3).

Whenever the Holy Spirit moves, powerful things always happen. Things truly change. He still takes dark things, such as pain and sorrow, and He makes them whole with His light of truth through His word. So many of us today are walking around with blank looks on our faces, emptiness in our hearts, and completely devoid of any purpose or plan.

What is the answer to this dilemma? We must allow the Holy Spirit to move upon our lives and give the light of His understanding to our hearts and minds so we will be led with His wisdom into God's plans and purposes for our lives. He loves to guide us and He will daily place His plan within our hearts.

We need to walk in the plans and ways of God, so the purpose for our lives can be fulfilled. It is sad that millions die without ever fully knowing the moving of the Spirit of Enlightenment upon their lives. It isn't because there is a lack of light; it's just a heart of rebellion that has chosen not to surrender to the One who made it.

The Holy Spirit is always listening. He always wants to make people and things into something good. He is the Spirit of creation and He longs to create. There is no lack of Him speaking; the only lack involves our receiving. This sounds so simple and we think we need something that is deeper and more complex. Why? It's because the flesh of man desires self-exaltation rather than spiritual exaltation, which is the result of our being seated in the heavenly position with Christ Jesus.

God is looking for people He can train to rule and reign in life with the authority He has given to us in Christ Jesus. What are some of the steps we need to take in order to learn to rule and reign?

1. Hand over the desire to be exalted.

2. Ask for the gift of a serving heart.

3. Be willing to be everything—or nothing—for the Lord alone.

4. Be willing to be pushed down—or lifted up—for the Lord alone.

5. Place your rights and your demands at the foot of the Cross.

6. Accept your role as an ambassador of Heaven, one who is full of truth, peace, and love.

7. Be found trustworthy in small things, as well as great things.

To be trustworthy is to be trusted and responsible and to be put under the care of the Kingdom of God. God is looking for trustworthy servants through whom He can reveal the Kingdom of God on earth to mankind. In other words, He is looking for pure, holy, open vessels through which His glory will flow.

He longs for us to become proclaimers of His Word. Therefore, let this promise from Ephesians become your personal proclamation: *"Blessed be the God and Father of our Lord Jesus Christ, who hath blessed us with all spiritual blessings in heavenly places in Christ. According as He hath chosen us in Him before the foundation of the world, that we should be holy and without blame before Him in love, having predestined us unto the adoption of the children by Jesus Christ to Himself according to good pleasure of His will, to the praise of the glory of his grace, wherein He hath made us accepted in the beloved"* (Eph. 1:3-6).

Chapter 23

Our Grace-Filled God

A Growing Garden of Grace

From the beginning, man has tried—and is still trying—to redeem himself. He works ever harder and longer, hoping he can work off his debts of sin and make everything right with God again. But the truth is, God's grace is always extended to every man, woman, and child. It seems strange that, with the job of redemption absolutely completed and finished, we still show up carrying our own toolbox, wanting to improve or add on to the absolutely accomplished, beautiful, and powerful work of the cross.

This kind of thinking reminds me of a person who goes to a beautiful ball, where everything is ready and waiting to be enjoyed, but because they did not have a part in the planning or implementation of it, they want to change this or that, so it has "their touch upon it."

God does not need "man's touch" in order to perfect what He has already perfected. The truth is that man needs God's touch and love.

In the beginning, the earth could not reach out to God. God had to reach out to earth in order to give it form and purpose. I think we would be closer to becoming the spotless Bride of Christ if we would remember that we all came from dirt to begin with. Dirt holds great potential. For that matter, we, too, hold great potential if we place ourselves in the hands of God so He can shape us into the people we were called to be. God wants to dirty His hands with man's dirt, so

He can wash them off in the basin of the blood of His Son, Jesus. His grace is more than enough to take our dirt and add love to it, and make a beautiful garden out of it.

The Song of Solomon reads, *"A garden enclosed is my sister, my spouse, a spring shut up, a fountain sealed"* (Song 4:12). What a beautiful description of the Bride, sealed by love and growing, because she carries a spring within in her a sealed fountain.

What do you carry within you? Do you really fully understand what (and Who) dwells within you? First, you must come to realize Who it is that resides within you. The name of the One who has chosen to dwell in you is the King of kings and Lord of lords: He is the King of glory.

In order to come to you, it cost Him everything. But at the same time, He deposited His eternal glory within you. This means that you carry the glory of God, and whenever and however the Spirit of God quickens you to move in His glory, you merely open yourself up and let the glory flow. This is simple for you to do, because you have already given over your right to hold onto any of your own glory. So now, as a free person, you have one thing to offer: His glory alone, so His name alone might be exalted.

You are now learning to walk fully in His name, for your name no longer needs to be exalted. You no longer have to believe in your own strength and in your own name and your own power, for you carry His.

THE SEAL OF THE HOLY SPIRIT

This is the tremendous gift that we carry within us—the glorified Savior. And now the Holy Spirit longs to let other people know the message and the power that is inherent in His Gospel. The Holy Spirit seals this message, as if it were the seal on an envelope containing a priceless document. The seal carries within it the greatest declarative proclamation of love that mankind will ever know.

He sealed this message in order to protect it with truth and love, but He has also opened the envelope and now declares—and wants us to declare with Him—the glorified Christ.

Jesus said, *"He that believeth on Me, as the Scripture hath said, out of his belly shall flow rivers of living water, but this spake he of the Spirit which they that believe on Him should receive, for the Holy Ghost was not given; because that Jesus was not yet glorified"* (John 7:38).

As believers we are sealed with the Holy Spirit of promise. Paul writes, *"In whom ye also trusted, after that ye heard the word of truth, the gospel of your salvation, in whom also after that ye believed, ye were sealed with that Holy Spirit of promise"* (Eph. 1:13). The Holy Spirit is the seal that guards us with grace, counsel, knowledge, might, wisdom, and understanding.

The Spirit of Grace will always be a 'grace-full' Spirit. Why? Because if we do not experience grace when we look at the cross and the pierced body of Jesus, we will become bitter and mourn, as one who has no hope or vision. God wants us always full of His grace, so we can know continued forgiveness and healing, for both ourselves and others.

The ancient prophet writes, *"And I will pour out upon the house of David and upon the inhabitants of Jerusalem the spirit of grace and of supplications, and they shall look upon Me whom they have pierced, and they shall mourn for Him as one mourneth for his only son and shall be in bitterness for Him, as one that is in bitterness for his firstborn"* (Zech. 12:10).

God always tries to reach us with the message of His love and His grace for us. How we respond will determine what our life and sometimes the lives of others will become.

I was puzzled about this Scripture from Zechariah and wondered what God was trying to tell us. Then I noticed what He said in the next verse, "In that day shall there be a great mourning in Jerusalem, as the mourning of Hadadrimmon in the valley of Megiddo." What happened in the valley of Megiddo? One event was the great loss of King Josiah. He was one of the good kings of Judah.

The full account of his story is found in Second Chronicles. He was born with the plans and purpose of God upon him. The Bible says, *"And, behold, there came a man of God out of Judah by the word of the LORD unto Bethel: and Jeroboam stood by the altar to burn incense. And he cried against the altar in the word of the LORD, and said, O altar, altar, thus saith the LORD; Behold, a child shall be born unto the house of David, Josiah by name; and upon thee shall he offer the priests of the high places that burn incense upon thee, and men's bones shall be burnt upon thee."* (1 Kings 13:1-2).

God had seen the sin and idolatry of men and was offering truth and grace under the rule of King Josiah, who was but a child when he began to reign in Jerusalem. The Chronicles describes him as follows, *"And he did that which was right in the sight of the Lord, and walked in the ways of David, his father, and declined neither to the right hand nor to the left. For in the eighth year of his reign he was yet young, he began to seek after the God of David, his father, and in the twelfth year he began to purge Judah and Jerusalem from the high places, and the groves, and the carved images, and the molten images"* (2 Chron. 34:2).

Josiah became a man who sought after the heart of God and the ways of God. The Bible goes on to record what he did to restore God's people and God's ways. That he brought them back to the heart of God is a matter of record. He purged the land and then went about repairing the house of the Lord. He brought the book of the Law, and he was committed to do all that it said to do. But there were few who felt as he did, and it broke his heart when he saw how far they had departed from the ways of God. He was so upset, in fact that he tore his garments.

This is what the Bible Quotes him as saying: *"Go, inquire of the LORD for me, and for them that are left in Israel and in Judah, concerning the words of the book that is found: for great is the wrath of the LORD that is poured out upon us, because our fathers have not kept the word of the LORD, to do after all that is written in this book"* (2 Chron. 34:21).

What a great witness that must have been to the people! Imagine if God's people today would have that in our hearts and we would proclaim it to others! To wholeheartedly take the Word of God and do all that it says to do out of love for the Lord is a message we need to proclaim and hear today. People are still people and sin is still sin, but God always has a great plan and way even if we His people don't fully reach out and accept it and take it to heart.

What a king Josiah must have been! He placed himself with his people. He wanted God's plan for himself and others. As I was reading about King Josiah, I couldn't help thinking about Jesus—how, long before He was born, the Prophet Isaiah spoke many prophecies about Him. In Isaiah 53, for example, the suffering of Jesus, His death, and victory for all mankind is so vividly described it was as if the Lord Himself had dictated it. Actually, he did so and it has been totally fulfilled.

The prophecy speaks of Jesus bearing the sins of mankind as He made intercession for the transgressors. King Josiah loved the Law and restored it, but King Jesus is the Word. The Gospel of John begins: *"In the beginning was the Word, and the Word was with God, and the Word was God"* (John 1:1). It all started in the very beginning, at the creation. The spoken Word of God formed and created everything but it is infinitely more powerful to *be* the Word as Jesus is. John goes on to say, *"And the Word was made flesh and dwelt among us, and we beheld his glory, the glory as of the only begotten of the Father, full of grace and truth"* (John 1:14).

Do you see the parallel between the earth that is void and waiting to be formed by the spoken Word, and the hovering of the Holy Spirit who brings the earth into its purpose and form? A virgin womb was waiting for someone to be formed within it. As the Holy Spirit hovered over Mary, she was made to fulfill the plans and purposes of God.

Chapter 24

Spirit of Grace

THE HOLY SPIRIT GUIDES YOU INTO TRUTH

So many today are like the earth was, void and without form. They are lifeless and empty. That is why the Holy Spirit hovers over the Word of God just as He does over the blood of Jesus.

When the Angel Gabriel came to Mary, He spoke the message of the plan of the Godhead for man's full redemption:

"And, behold thou shalt conceive in thy womb and bring forth a son and shalt call His name Jesus. He shall be great and shall be called the son of the Highest and the Lord God shall give unto Him the throne of His father David. And He shall reign over the house of Jacob forever, and of His kingdom their shall be no end. Then Mary said unto the angel, how shall this be, seeing I know not a man? And the angel answered and said unto her, 'The Holy Ghost shall come upon thee, and the power of the Highest shall overshadow thee; therefore, also that holy thing which shall be born in thee shall be called the Son of God" (Luke 1:31-33).

The Holy Spirit is the overseer of the Word of God, just as He was the overseer of the Covenant. God in His infinite wisdom knew that man himself would never be able to keep himself from all sin—maybe from some, but not from all. The Bible says, *"For all have sinned and come short of the glory of God"* (Rom. 3:23). This is a truth you can see even in the lives of children, you have to teach them the ways of the Lord.

The way we see sin is not how God sees sin. John writes, *"If we say that we have no sin, we deceive ourselves, and truth is not in us"* (1 John 1:8). How does the truth get in to us? Go back to what Jesus said, *"Even the Spirit of truth; whom the world cannot receive, because it seeth him not, neither knoweth him, but ye know him; for he dwelleth with you, and shall be in you"* (John 14:17).

This truth was so important that Jesus repeated it: *"Howbeit when He, the Spirit of truth, is come, He will guide you into the truth, for He shall not speak of Himself; but whatsoever He shall hear, that shall He speak: and He will show you things to come"* (John 16:13). The Holy Spirit is neither deaf nor dumb, even if some men treat Him as if he were. He hears and He longs to speak, while He shows us the truth.

What was Jesus saying here? Does the Holy Spirit hear the words spoken between the members of the Godhead? Of course He does! After all, He is the third person of the Godhead.

The Godhead has a holy, eternal mission toward man, but will mankind show up and respond to Them? Will mankind receive Their gift of salvation?

When Jesus was 12, not yet a teenager, He started doing His Father's business—He was pursuing the mission and mandate of the Trinity. *"And He said unto them, how is that ye sought me? Wist ye not that I must be about my Father's business? And they understood not the saying which He spake unto them"* (Luke 2:49).

Mary and Joseph wanted answers. After all, their son had been missing for three days. Later on, He would go missing for another three days, when He once again was doing His Father's business. When He returned, He had conquered all the dominions of hell.

I wonder if Mary remembered the first time when her son was gone for three days. Did she hear the echoing voice of her 12-year-old saying, "I must be about my Father's business?" He is still about His Father's business today.

Thank you, Jesus! What a tremendous vision we can hold onto! Jesus is praying for us, the Holy Spirit is praying for us when we don't know how to pray, and one forever-loving Father is always ready to hear and answer the cries of His children.

THE PRICE OF GRACE

Yes, Jesus fulfilled the Law. Paul writes, *"There is therefore now no condemnation to them which are in Christ Jesus, who walked not after the flesh, but after the Spirit. For the law of the Spirit of life in Christ Jesus hath made me free from the law of sin and death. For what the law could not do, in that it was weak through the flesh, God sending His own Son in the likeness of sinful flesh, and for sin, condemned sin in the flesh. That the righteousness of the law might be fulfilled in us, who walked not after the flesh, but after the Spirit"* (Rom. 8:1-4). God knew what man was made of. He gave us fleshly bodies with a free will. He also knew if we would grasp the knowledge of man being a sinner, saved by grace, we would be able to live our lives in Christ Jesus. As free-willed people who are innately self-centered, we fight His grace with our pride. Do we want His grace? If we do, we must humble ourselves in order to receive it.

To live in grace, we must stay at the foot of the cross and see always before us the price of grace. It is impossible to have a lot of pride in yourself when you gaze up at someone else who was able to do for you what you were unable to do for yourself.

That is humility, and it is the antidote for pride. We want so badly to add to the finished work of the death of Jesus on the cross. We may never openly admit it, but we show it. How? One of the most common ways is to take credit for answered prayers by saying "I" prayed for that. The truth is, God poured out the Spirit of supplication at the same time He poured out the Spirit of grace.

WHAT IS THE SPIRIT OF GRACE?

The Spirit of grace is powerful, yet absolutely simple. Grace, in the final analysis, is extended love—the action of a loving, all-knowing God, reaching out with His love and power to a helpless, prideful, lost people, though they do not receive or want it.

Grace is freely offered and given to all.

Grace remains steadfast in love. Grace demands truth for it to be received and understood.

Grace is a gift, based on what is in the heart of the Giver, not the receiver.

Grace is a working agent that must be applied in order for it to be effective.

Grace goes beyond the needs—and sometimes even the wants—of the receiver.

Grace is power and strength that is offered from Someone greater than the receiver.

Grace, freely given, can expire, for the One who gives it controls where, when, and how it will be imparted and distributed.

Grace can be made null and void if the person to whom it is extended rejects it. Grace honors free will and free choices.

Grace brings spiritual freedom as a gift, many times coming in a package that contains other gifts as well.

Grace also carries hope, joy, peace, power, understanding, truth, and life within it.

Grace shines brightly during the darkest night.

Grace establishes God's plan and fulfills God's purpose.

Grace gives birth to humility.

Grace carries life within it and is able to bring back to life what once was dead.

Grace, born of life, is stronger than death.

Grace becomes effective when it becomes embraced.

Picture a person who is so weak that he or she is unable to lift up, or open their hands to receive; such a person is bound by someone or something. This individual is trapped and dying even if he or she does not know it or care about it. It is then grace that enters in and causes a reaction. It brings life.

Chapter 25

The Law Demands

JESUS IS THE TRUTH

Grace offers life but wrath brings death. We now are under God's grace, whether we understand it or accept it. Our choices do not change the truth. The Bible tells us, *"For the grace of God that bringeth salvation hath appeared to all men"* (Titus 2:11). God made provision for all men. By offering them His grace, He made the possibility of salvation available to all, forever.

As I was growing up I was taught about grace, but like so many of us I never really understood it. Guilt was the leader, and fear was the rear guard. The best we could hope for was what King David hoped for. *"Surely goodness and mercy shall follow me all the days of my life, and I shall dwell in the house of the Lord forever"* (Ps. 23:6). But grace cannot do its work if the heart it wants to encourage is filled with guilt and fear.

Religion, without the understanding and message of grace, brings fear and pride. We try and try to do better, but all we get better at is justifying ourselves—in our own eyes and the eyes of others.

That is not of God for God sent love and grace to us to deliver us from the bondage of sin. It came embodied in truth and His name is Jesus.

The opposite of grace is a law that is impossible to fulfill, no matter how hard we try. The Law shows you what you have done wrong whether it is your fault or not. The Law demands full payment, and it is totally indifferent to your ability to pay. The Law can change its demands, yet it must still be paid. Those under the Law have no say in what and when and how they should pay. The Law demands full and immediate payment, even to the point of death.

For those who are laboring under the Law, there is hope. It is in the form of grace released by God, and it can give us the ability to live within the law in a respectful way.

A few days before one Christmas I was at home when a friend called me. She and her husband needed help leaving another friend's car at the airport for her, so that when she and her husband returned, their car would be waiting for them. "I don't know the ins and outs of the airport, Eileen, so will you go with us she asked?"

I agreed, and in a few minutes my friend and her husband pulled up in the car that was to be dropped off. I got in my car and led them to the airport. All was well. At the airport I pulled in at the arrival gate, waiting in my car for her husband, who had taken their friend's car to the short-term parking lot.

The airport was very busy that day with lots of people coming home or going home for the holidays. The sidewalk in front of the arrival door was crowded with people who were attempting to maneuver around each another with oversized suitcases. Though I was not in the crosswalk, I was close to it, and I thought I would just back up, to give people a little more room to walk.

I looked in my side mirror and the rearview mirror, then shifted into reverse and hit a car I hadn't seen. In fact, even after I hit it, I didn't see it. But I'd heard it, all right! It made a kind of a *smunchy,* broken-glass sound.

Embarrassed and a little numb, I got out of my car and went back to survey the damage. My car was all right; there was just another little scrape to go with the others back there. No big deal. The other person's car, however, did not fare quite as well—it had a broken parking light and some paint damage.

We exchanged the necessary information, and I assured the other person that I would pay for the repair. "Just let me know how much it is, and I'll take care of it. I'm really sorry about this; I had no idea you were there," I explained.

We had finished the necessary business and as I was getting back into my car, the law arrived in the form of a security woman. According to the law, when you back up and hit someone, you are supposed to get a ticket. She ushered us all into her office, where we filled out a report. Never having been in a situation like this before, I had no idea how the legal system worked. She gave me a ticket and told me to appear in court on a certain day at a certain time.

When I got home, I studied the ticket. Actually, it gave me two options: I could mail the ticket in with $40 and have two points added to my driving record, or I could appear in court. I did not even know where 'court' was, but I did know that if you accumulated enough points, you could lose your license. I'd never received any points, and I wasn't about to accept any now.

So now came the really important decision: what to wear to court. What would make me not look real guilty and help me find favor? I settled on a navy blue outfit, because I knew it was a safe color.

At the appointed hour, I asked Fred to come with me for moral support. My day in court was truly memorable. First, they showed a video of our legal rights and explained the different ways we could plead. That was a no-brainer; I was guilty, and I had to admit it. (God was watching you know.)

When the clerk called my name, I raised my hand, feeling decidedly queasy. I could certainly recognize the need for something bigger than us holding us accountable and keeping us safe, but I did not like the idea of the entire state being against me.

Someone handed me a paper. It was a plea-bargain form. Because I had a good driving record, it explained, I would receive only one point on my record. But I would still have to pay the minimum fine of 40 dollars. All I had to do was sign the form and pay, and I would be free to go.

I shook my head. My driving record was impeccable, and I wanted to keep it that way.

In response to my decision, I received a frown from the official along with a terse explanation. He explained that a city district attorney across the hall would talk to me.

As I entered the attorney's office with the plea bargain in my hand, he pointed to it. "That's the minimum and it's our best offer."

Remembering I was guilty, I meekly nodded. "All right."

He went on, "To reduce this to one point, we're going to have to rewrite the charge. We'll make it for driving with a defective front headlight."

I bit my lip. This was not the time to point out there was nothing wrong with my headlights. I agreed to the false charge, realizing that the law must be satisfied, regardless of the truth. Why? Because it was the law.

Laws were necessary for our protection, to guide the flesh in what was right and wrong. And to be effective laws have to carry with them some form of punishment.

Had I failed to appear or send in my fine, I would have been cited for contempt of court. The law went after you for this is the way it maintained its power.

Have you ever been driving along and seen a patrol car in the traffic behind you? In all probability, your first response is to glance down to make sure you're not speeding. The officer behind you may have the motto "To serve and protect" on the side of his car, but he also represents the law, and he is its enforcer. The law only works if it has the power to force compliance.

With grace, however, it is a different matter. It is the spirit behind it which gives it its power. Grace with action and power is the love of God toward us, His people. Just as the law stepped in and gave me a ticket for an illegal act, when Heaven steps in it becomes an act of love and grace is the "citation" we receive.

Chapter 26

The Longing Overseer

The Intent of Grace

The grace of God is always there, ready to be reinforced for us but we need to be identified with it. The Bible says, *"For wages of sin is death, but the gift of God is eternal life through Jesus Christ our Lord"* (Rom. 6:23).

We've become so familiar with this verse that we sometimes loose the intent of it. Just as there is always intent behind a law, there is intent behind grace. An intentional, loving God is making a way for His precious people, you and me. God wants us all to find and live in grace freely, in close relationship with Him. He provided grace for us in Jesus, and now He wants us to allow the Holy Spirit to establish that revelation in us. Paul writes, *"Thou therefore, my son, be strong in the grace that is in Christ Jesus."* (2 Tim. 2:1).

It would seem, therefore, according to the Word that we need to come into Jesus and His grace, and let His grace do its work in us. Only in that way will we become full partakers of His grace, according to His provision.

Sin and death leave us spiritually comatose, but then the Holy Spirit breathes life into our dead bodies. He takes the grave clothes of sin off of us, and in their place He clothes us in the righteous robe of Jesus. At the same time we are covered in His grace. The Bible says, *"I delight greatly in the Lord. My soul rejoices in my God. For he has clothed me with the garment of salvation and arrayed me in a robe of righteousness"* (Isa. 61:10).

Why did Jesus leave His grave clothes behind? Perhaps it was to remind us that we need to put them on—to put on Christ Jesus and be wrapped in Him, His salvation gift, and the power He provided for us. Maybe He wants us to be able to come before His Father and ours wearing "His leftover bloody clothing, that have now become our shining robes of His righteousness."

John writes, *"Both were running, but the other disciple outran Peter and reached the tomb first. He bent over and looked in at the strips of linen lying there but did not go in. Then Simon Peter, who was behind him, arrived and went into the tomb. He saw the strips of linen lying there, as well as the burial cloth that had been around Jesus' head. The cloth was folded by itself, separate from the linen"* (John 20:4-7).

Jesus left His blood-stained grave clothes behind so we could come totally into His identity and be clothed in Him. Why was the napkin that was about His head set aside, separated from the other grave clothes? Could the napkin be a reminder to each person that we must use our own free wills and decide if we want to be clothed in what He left us to wear: The bloody robes of His righteousness, hemmed in His grace, and full of His love!

John was the first deciple to believe that Jesus had risen from the dead. The others went back to their homes. God still honors each person and gives grace, yet He never controls man's choice. Notice what John says: *"Then the disciples went back to their homes, but Mary stood outside the tomb crying. As she wept, she bent over to look into the tomb and she saw two angels in white, seated where Jesus body had been, one at the head and the other at the foot. They asked her "Woman why are you crying?" "They have taken my Lord away," she said, "and I don't know where they put him." And at this, she turned around and saw Jesus standing there, but she did not recognize that it was Jesus. "Woman," He said, "why are you crying? Who is it you are looking for?" Thinking he was the gardener she said, "Sir if you have carried him away, tell me where you have put him, and I will get him. Then Jesus said to her "Mary"* (John 20:10-16).

Mary did not recognize Jesus in the Garden until He spoke her name. He loved her so much that He had positioned Himself to be found by her.

CLOTHED WITH POWER FROM ON HIGH

After we call upon the name of the Lord, He calls back our name. What a sound of joy must ring throughout Heaven when a searching heart cries out to Jesus! What a triumphant sound must be heard on high—and perhaps, a sigh of relief—when the Book of Life has a new name entered into it! How all Heaven longs to clothe us and place a new name upon us!

We are called "overcomers." This is a new identity that is full of life and removes all death. Jesus said, *"He that overcometh, the same clothed in white raiment: and I will not blot out his name out of the book of life, but I will confess his name before my Father, and before his angels"* (Rev. 3:5). What pleasure it brings the Godhead to see Their offer of eternal life accepted! It must bless Them to see the creation longing to have fellowship with Them again!

The Shepherd longs to have His sheep recognize His voice. He wants us to come to Him on a first-name basis, and He calls each of us by name. Jesus said, *"My sheep listen to my voice; and I know them, and they follow me. I will give them eternal life, and they shall never perish; no one can snatch them out of my hand. My Father, who has given them to me, is greater than all, no one can snatch them out of my Fathers hand. I and the Father are one"* (John 10:27-30 NIV) What a comfort it is to know God never discards us and He always honors the free will that He has given to us.

How shall we be clothed with this power from on high? In the same way His followers were. They waited, worshiping Him, and were full of great joy and awesome anticipation. They knew something new and different was about to happen, though they had no idea what it was. They did know one thing for sure: they were to stay together in unity and agreement, continuously praising God at the Temple, until they entered into the upper room and experienced being clothed with power from on high.

It was a matter of choice then, and it is the same today. How do you want to follow Jesus and His ways? How close to Him do you want to be?

The Father sent the Holy Spirit to teach us His ways and to clothe us with power from on high. Jesus said, *"I am going to send you what my Father has promised; but stay in the city until you have been clothed with power from on high"* (Luke 24:49 NIV). We can choose to be fully clothed in God's power and ways, or we can choose to be only partially clothed by being open only occasionally to wearing His power and ways under certain circumstances.

Which type of person are you? Do you want partial power? A partial covering? Are you willing to serve Him on Sunday morning, but not today? Not right now? The Word says that, "we go from glory to glory in Christ Jesus" (2 Cor. 3:18).

We are offered the position of glory in Jesus, yet if we still long to fulfill our flesh via our self-will, selfishness, rebellion, and self-centeredness we will always be away from Jesus and His offer of glory. He wants us to remain open, so we can receive His whole gift of abundant and everlasting life, right now, right here on earth. To be open to the ways and changes God offers us all is a wonderful gift and it requires us to be vulnerable. Ask God for this gift and for His grace to be able to receive it.

Paul writes, *"But we all, with opened face beholding as in a glass the glory of the Lord, are changed into the same image from glory to glory, even as 'by' the Spirit of the Lord"* (2 Cor. 3:18). The question is, are we in close enough fellowship with the Lord to be changed by Him? If we long to be changed into the image of Jesus, we need to have the same intimate walk with the Holy Spirit that Jesus had. We need to be pliable so the Holy Spirit can mold us for the glory of God regardless of the approval of man.

The Holy Spirit burns with zeal and love for Jesus. He wants the glory of Jesus to be upon believers, so the world will see Jesus, as they behold "those who believe in Him."

Jesus made full provision for us now and forever. He longs to clothe us in His own power and glory. We need only stand still and be found at the foot of His cross. His death and blood are the inner garments we love to wear and His glory is the outer garment we wear for the world to see and desire. We are walking, talking, living displays of the glory of God.

Paul wrote these words to the believers in Corinth, *"Ye are our epistle written in our hearts, known and read of all men: Forasmuch as ye are manifestly declared to be the epistle of Christ ministered by us, written not with ink, but with the Spirit of the living God; not in tables of stone, but in fleshly tables of the heart"* (2 Cor. 3:2-3).

And the next verse reads, *"And such trust have we through Christ to God-ward: Not that we are sufficient of ourselves to think any thing as of ourselves; but our sufficiency is of God; Who also hath made us able ministers of the new testament; not of the letter, but of the spirit: for the letter killeth, but the spirit giveth life"* (2 Cor. 3:4-6).

We need to get this truth out of our heads and move it deeper into our hearts. It has been said that the Kingdom of Self is located 18 inches north and slightly east of the Kingdom of God. As long as the truth stays in our heads only, it will never change our lives. We need to be like Mary, within our hearts, asking the Holy Spirit to take our stony hearts and change them into soft, warm hearts that beat for the glory of God.

Why did Jesus leave His grave clothes and the napkin that was wrapped around His head? He could have made them disappear. What was He was saying to us in doing this? Could it be that what is of earth should stay on earth, and what is of glory should go to glory? Could He have left His head napkin, so we might use it as a face cloth to wash our own faces in His glorious blood? To make them open to receive His glory and His love?

God promises, *"Now the Lord is the spirit, and where the spirit of the Lord is, there is freedom. And we who with unveiled faces all reflect the Lord's glory, are being transformed into His likeness with everlasting glory, which comes from the Lord, who is the spirit"* (2 Cor. 3:17 NIV).

Chapter 27

Your Inheritance

Just as Moses when he was clothed with the glory of God had to put a veil over His face to keep its radiance hidden from the people, now the time has come for us to show our faces shining with the glory of God to others. It is a glorious day for those who fully embrace the glory of God and His Spirit! He wants His people to have open and radiant faces, so people can see the glory of God and want to have it for themselves. Jesus wants his people to have open faces that are full of the reflection of the glory of Calvary and Heaven.

The phrase "Spirit of the Lord" connotes divine ownership. The Godhead has always been in one accord, and now They reach out to us, offering us the opportunity to become a thread that can be woven into the Godhead, just as the Three are woven into each other as One. They extend a blood-written invitation to us and await our reply. What will your reply be?

Oh what a glorious love You share!

Come, Holy Spirit, stay down here.

Open my heart, open my mind,

let me know You all of the time.

Help me to follow my Savior and Lord
for You alone stay in one accord.

One accord with the Father,
one accord with the Son
now on earth, striving with man.

What is the cord that you placed on me?

Could it be
the one that held my King's robe,
as He walked toward His death
was holding onto the vision of me?

Oh, my friend, my wonderful Guide
I want to stoop down and look closely inside.
I want to see His grave clothes folded neatly inside.
I want You to clothe me, with my Groom's clothes
that He provided for me, His Bride.

I bow my head down.
Please place His head napkin on mine
so I can understand all of God's plan.

Help me to see and know the power inside,

for You alone can tell what they carry inside.

I know they were used to wrap my beloved Groom,

but He was from Heaven and they were from earth,

so He left them from His death for my new birth.

I only know that when Heaven came down,

nothing could stop Him or hold Him down.

Open my eyes and let me see

my glorious Savior, risen and free.

Yes, the Father wants to pass on to others the bloody, hand-me-downs of Jesus, and the Holy Spirit is there, being the Overseer of the wardrobe. He goes to the divine closet of grace and takes the bloody robes off the three nail hooks that came from the wooden cross at Calvary and goes to and fro, looking for those who will allow Him to dress them. He longs to explain to them how greatly they are valued so they can treasure themselves as He does.

Does the Holy Spirit want His own glory? Never! He wants man to become the glory of Jesus and would have us know that we are the treasured inheritance of Jesus.

The glory of God is the lifter of our heads, so our gaze will be fixed on Heaven. The Psalmist writes, *"But thou, O Lord, art a shield for me; my glory, and the lifter up of mine head"* (Ps. 3:3).

The Holy Spirit was sent that we might see through enlightened eyes all that Jesus has done for us, that we might see His provision for us while we are still here but looking toward Heaven. Our heavenly Counselor and Guide desires to explain our inheritance, and the price Jesus has paid for it. What inheritance? It is not *what*, but *Who*. The

Lord Jesus! The Bible says, *"The LORD is the portion of mine inheritance and of my cup: thou maintainest my lot"* (Ps 16:5).

He, in turn, has inherited us, and He has sent an Overseer to us who longs to fellowship with us, just as Jesus fellowshipped with His Father while on earth.

Now Jesus has sent us an invitation written in His blood inviting us to come alongside the Overseer and declare with one voice, "Jesus is Lord!"

The Spirit and the Bride say "Come!"

Let him who hears, say, "Come!"

Whoever is thirsty, let him come!

Whoever wishes, let him take the free gift of the water of life (Rev. 22:17).

Are you thirsty? Are you standing by the Holy Spirit?

Are you crying out with the Holy Spirit saying, "Come, Lord Jesus, come?"

Are you wishing to take freely of the gift of the water of life?

If so, no longer wish, but choose! Choose right now—this day, this moment—to start to drink in the Spirit of the Lord.

Once you begin to drink from the water of life, then you, too, will begin to say, "Come Lord Jesus, come!"

When this happens you will be hidden away, covered in the blood of Jesus, and wearing the robes of righteousness. You will hear the echo that rings out through all eternity, and it will cause your heart to leap, for it will be the voice of your beloved Jesus, your Savior, *"Yes, I am coming soon."*

He will hear the echo of the Spirit of the Lord and you will cry out "Amen. Come, Lord Jesus!"

For the Spirit of the Lord will plant deep in your heart the grace of the Lord Jesus Christ that is to be with God's people. The day and the hour are approaching. Whether it be today or a 1,000 years from now, the day will come when you will hear the voice of the King cry out:

> *"Behold! I am coming soon! My reward is with me, and I will give to everyone according to what he has done. I am the Alpha and the Omega, the First and the Last, the Beginning and the End"* **(Rev. 22, 12:13, NIV).**

Additional copies of this book and other book titles from DESTINY IMAGE are available at your local bookstore.

Call toll-free: 1-800-722-6774.

Send a request for a catalog to:

Destiny Image® **Publishers, Inc.**
P.O. Box 310
Shippensburg, PA 17257-0310

*"Speaking to the Purposes of God for This
Generation and for the Generations to Come"*

**For a complete list of our titles,
visit us at www.destinyimage.com**